Children & Divorce

Children & Divorce

WHAT TO EXPECT
HOW TO HELP

Archibald D. Hart, Ph.D.

WORD BOOKS
PUBLISHER
WACO, TEXAS

A DIVISION OF
WORD, INCORPORATED

CHILDREN AND DIVORCE:
WHAT TO EXPECT, HOW TO HELP

Library of Congress catalog card number: 82-550515
ISBN 0-8499-0313-0

Scripture quotations marked NEB are from *The New English
Bible*, © The Delegates of the Oxford University
Press and the Syndics of the Cambridge University
Press, 1961, 1970, used by permission. All other Scripture
quotations are from the King James Version of the Bible.

Printed in the United States of America

To

GERTRUDE AND HENRY

*I will forever be thankful for the
life you gave to me.*

Contents

Preface

ARE THE CHILDREN OF DIVORCE any different from other children? On the outside they don't appear to be. They laugh, cry, wear the latest crazes, and watch the same television shows as other children. But are they different?

I believe they are, and I am speaking from personal experience as well as from professional knowledge. My parents were divorced when I was twelve years of age, and I know that my life was changed forever because of their breakup. As a psychotherapist I have also worked with many divorcing and divorced families, and my experience has convinced me that the children of divorced parents are indeed different from other children—for divorce, although no longer the stigma it once was, is nevertheless a wrenching, painful, unfortunate series of events that imposes on children adjustments and changes they often are not capable of making. In my practice I have seen enough to convince me that divorce is the most serious and complex mental health crisis facing the children of the eighties.

The reports of researchers in this area back up what I have concluded from my own experience—that the effects of divorce on children are far more serious and long-lasting than most divorced parents are willing to admit to themselves. For example, studies released in England in 1978 show that children of divorce have a shorter life expectancy and more illness than children from intact families; they also leave school earlier. In New York City, where more suicides occur during adolescence than at any other time of life, two out of every three teenage suicides come from broken homes. Even those children whose reactions are less dramatic often struggle well into adulthood with repressed anger, anxiety, and depression stemming from the time of their parents' divorce.

This is not to say that these children are always irrevocably damaged or emotionally crippled as a result of divorce. It is possible, I suppose, that in a few instances these children have become better-adjusted adults as a consequence of their experience. But is the risk worth it? If they are reasonably well adjusted now, could they have been even better adjusted without having to go through a family breakup? What did the adjustment cost them in time, effort, and possibly money paid for therapy or counseling? No one will ever know for sure, because these are issues that frequently elude research strategies.

Are the children of Christian parents any better off in a divorce? I believe not. If anything, I would venture to suggest that in many instances they are in a worse situation. Why? In addition to all the problems that a child has to face in adjusting to the breakup of one home and the possible creation of another, the child of Christian parents has to confront the failure of their religious system to resolve the problem of conflict in the home. The child has to confront questions such as: "Why didn't God intervene and save the family from destruction?" "Why doesn't God answer my prayers?" "Does Christianity really work?" "Are my parents really Christians? If they are, why can't they work out their problems?" In the process, the child can become disillusioned with Christianity, and may seriously question whether spiritual values are helpful or important.

The purpose of this book is to provide help for parents (and for other concerned adults, such as grandparents, friends, and teachers) in minimizing the damaging effects of divorce on children. It is written from a Christian perspective and directed primarily at Christian parents, because I am of the opinion that the children of such parents are at greater risk than others. The eternal consequences of Christian parents' being stumbling blocks to their children weigh heavily on my mind. I don't believe that Christians can hide behind the old adage that children are flexible enough to learn to cope and "bounce back" from events as traumatic as a marital breakup. The least we as concerned adults can do is to ensure that the impact of the divorce on children's mental and spiritual health is kept to a minimum. This book seeks to address the important issues at stake, to show what it feels like to be a child of divorce, to deal with the major risk factors, and to offer suggestions for alleviating the damaging consequences divorce is likely to have on children.

I want to make it clear that, in offering help to these children and their parents, I am in no way recommending or condoning divorce. Neither am I seeking to add to anyone's burden of guilt. I am assuming that many divorces are, for whatever reason, inevitable. If, however, after reading this book, someone who is contemplating divorce decides to seek further help in saving his or her marriage, I will be extremely pleased, because a secondary purpose of this book is to communicate just how serious the consequences of divorce can be for children, and to remind parents of the rights children have whenever a family breakup is contemplated.

If you are considering divorce, for whatever reason, I urge you to read this book before you take any further steps. Divorce is a sad indictment against our culture; despite progress in so many areas we still can't teach people how to live together. And if divorce is sad for people in general, it is infinitely more pathetic for Christians, who claim to have at their disposal all the resources of a great and loving God.

If, however, your divorce cannot be avoided, or if you divorced before you became a Christian, or if you are divorced for no reason of your own—if you are the unwilling victim of circumstances—then I trust you will also find comfort in this book. As you work through its principles and apply the help offered, I pray that you will be among those who have been able to turn apparent disaster into meaningful growth. Use this book in your personal devotions, small study groups, or as a family guide. My prescription is that you use it with a large dose of God's forgiveness. He is the only sure source of healing for the pain, guilt, and resentment divorce brings, and he is also a dependable source of strength in the struggle to bring children through the divorce experience with a minimum of damage.

ARCHIBALD D. HART

1

Divorced at Twelve

MY MOTHER KEPT TELLING ME, "It's not the end of the world." But how do you convince a child of twelve that the breakup of his family is not the end of everything secure and stable? We were packing our suitcases. My brother, Kenny, only ten years of age, seemed less bothered than I. He had already developed a reputation for being tough. He never cried. My parents could spank him and he would never flinch. The sight of suitcases spread around my mother's bedroom even excited him, as if it meant we were leaving home to go on some adventure. In typical older-brother fashion I said to myself, "He's too young to understand what is happening. I'll handle this for both of us."

I was frantic. How could my mother be doing this? Had she gone crazy? I knew that she had been unhappy for a long time, but how was running away going to solve anything? I tried pleading with her. Would she reconsider her actions? Couldn't she see I was frightened? She replied that I didn't understand— that I was too young to know about these things.

The pain in my chest got worse. My head felt as if it was going to explode; ideas for making her see reason were falling over one another. Suddenly I felt old for my years, as if I was being called upon to carry a burden that was too heavy for me. Then I felt childish and helpless again. I started to cry, softly at first, and then my sobs became angry screams directed at my mother. I told her that I hated her, but she only ignored me. She knew how to handle hysterical people. Softly she told me to hurry up with my packing. "Make sure you take everything you need for school. I don't intend coming back here to fetch anything you forget." I knew she meant business, so reluctantly I complied, even though I felt that leaving home was the end of the world for me.

I can't remember exactly what happened after that. I know my heart ached as if I were having a heart attack. I believe I became quiet as I realized how pointless my resistance was.

My mother had not directly come out and said, "I'm going to divorce your father." She merely presented it as wanting to live away from him. Either she wasn't very clear in her own mind about what she wanted to do, or she was protecting us from further hurt by taking the divorce in stages. But I knew what was happening, and the fact that she was not being honest only made it worse for me.

Why Divorce?

My mother and father had been fighting for many years. Even now, as I reflect back on their marriage, I don't fully understand why. Partly, I believe, it was that they married too young, before their adult personalities had fully formed; they plainly just outgrew each other. Partly it was that they were unable to communicate clearly to each other, to talk through conflicts over relatively minor issues to the point of understanding and agreement. Partly it was that they were both very insecure. This made them extremely jealous of each other, and as a result they each became very possessive and controlling. There was no freedom and little happiness in their relationship.

One question often haunts me. Would their marriage have survived if they had been Christians—I mean real Christians? They were nominal church attenders and saw to it that my brother and I went to Sunday school regularly. They advocated honesty and valued sincerity. But they knew nothing of a God who could take control of their hurts and help them give and receive forgiveness. They knew nothing about prayer, and could not have found a word of promise or encouragement from Scripture even if they had wanted to. Could they have survived if they had known how to use these resources? I believe they could have! Yet I see many Christian marriages that don't survive. I suppose if you are thirsty it is not enough to carry a bucket of water. You must also know how to drink!

The Emotional Aftereffects

In the months after we left the house, we lived first in a hotel and then in an apartment. My father was grief-stricken. He tried everything to make amends to my mother, but she would not give in. Finally, the divorce went through.

During this time I was very unhappy. I lost interest in my hobbies, I didn't want to go to school, and I became pessimistic about the future. Nothing seemed to matter to me. I began to do things that bothered my parents, such as failing to tie my shoe-laces. I suspect that this was a way of getting attention from my mother; untied shoelaces make a "clickity-click" sound as you slop around, and sooner or later someone notices. My irritating behavior took other forms as well. My socks began appearing in unmatched pairs, and no matter how I tried I seemed to be late for everything—meals, school, and music lessons.

In retrospect, I can see that much of my behavior was an attempt to punish my parents for their actions. If they could see how troubled I was, I thought to myself, perhaps they would come together again and we would live happily ever after. It didn't happen, of course. By and large my behaviors were ignored. My mother was too preoccupied with her own emotional pain and had little energy left to deal with mine.

Gradually I gave up on the manipulative maneuvers and gave in to a genuine feeling of grief. I was in mourning just as if someone I loved had died; the full reality of the divorce had finally hit home. The pain which up to this point had seemed to be in my chest now settled in my stomach. I didn't know it, but the process of healing had begun.

I can't recall how long my grieving lasted. I suppose the intense part was over in three or four weeks, but this was followed by a low-level depression that must have lasted for a long time.

Actually, the grieving process came in spasms. First there was the major grief reaction over the loss of the family unit, but this was followed by a series of awarenesses of the other losses that go with being divorced. Some of these I became aware of only in the months and years that followed. For instance, let me list just a few of the losses I experienced:

—loss of my home;

—loss of my neighborhood friends;

—loss of convenient transportation (we only had one automobile in the family);

—dramatic reduction in our standard of living;

—loss of family outings together.

These were all tangible losses to me. Many others were more abstract and therefore more difficult to identify, but they contributed their share to the pain I felt.

One of the painful necessities I had to face during this time was telling my friends about the divorce. Divorce, while becoming more common, still had a stigma attached to it, and the children of our neighborhood still tended to react out of fear of the unknown. The reaction of my friends was far from sympathetic. They seemed to panic as much as I did, and this added to my pain and fear.

At night, while I was trying to go to sleep, my imagination would have a field day; my mind would feed me all sorts of ridiculous ideas. I would fantasize, for instance, that somehow my parents would get back together, and I would picture our united family smiling together. But most of my fantasies were more negative. I would imagine I was grown up and looking for employment. In the job interview I would be asked, "Are you a divorced child?" I would have to reply, "Yes, I am," and would then be told, "I'm sorry, but we don't have a position for you." It seems crazy, but that's what a mind does when it is bothered.

My worst fantasy was that I would never have a girlfriend. I was just beginning to see girls as necessary and desirable and not as nuisances. One girl in my school class had attracted my attention. She seemed friendly toward me and invited me to her home to meet her parents. But what would they think if they knew I was a divorced child? Could I keep it a secret from them? What would happen if they eventually found out? I withdrew from her friendship to avoid embarrassment and hurt, and I resolved to live the rest of my life as a hermit.

While I didn't quite become a recluse, I did shun social contacts for a while. I became very self-conscious, convinced that everybody was looking at me—talking about me and my family. I feared that they were shunning me as if I were diseased. I can clearly remember listening with rapt attention in Sunday school to the story of Jesus healing the leper. I knew exactly what it was like to be an outcast and to warn everybody of your presence so that they would not be contaminated by your disease. I felt like a divorce leper!

Feelings for Mother

When my mother first took us away from home, I directed all my anger at her. She was, after all, the one who initiated the family breakup. In my rage, I wanted to humiliate her, even physically hurt her.

It is very hard for a child with such feelings to think clearly. I was oblivious to my mother's pain; I thought only of myself and how her actions were going to affect me. This is, after all, the natural self-preservation instinct God has built into each of us. The security of a family and the assurance of stability is essential for all of us, but especially for a child. We need a haven from the storms of growing up, a harbor in which we can build a vessel strong enough to brave the storms of a cruel and unstable world. When this security is threatened, every protective instinct God has created in us is mobilized. It is no wonder, therefore, that divorce makes a child so angry!

When the separation between my parents was formally established and my brother and I began to visit our father, my anger toward my mother turned to feelings of hate. I became disrespectful, trying to make sure she knew how much she had hurt me and how she was destroying our lives. Sometimes I refused to speak to her, using silence as a weapon. She was entirely to blame, I felt, not for the misery in the marriage (I was fully aware of my father's contribution to this), but for initiating the breakup.

But the worst was yet to come. Shortly after the divorce was finalized, my mother announced that she was getting married again. I felt that my destruction was now complete. The fantasies of reconciliation were shattered. My conscious wish and prayer that somehow God was going to pull off a miracle and unite us all again vanished into thin air. Once again feelings of despair and hopelessness set in. I had known nothing of my mother's courting. (She had started seeing another man shortly after the separation). But it was clear to me that this new relationship was driving the final nails into the divorce coffin. I felt like I was the one inside!

Feelings for Father

Through the early years of my childhood I had developed a love-hate relationship with my father. I admired many of his skills; I believed he could build anything, repair anything—do anything. He was fun to play with. His stories about his childhood and teenage exploits enthralled my brother and me. I would rather have heard him tell of his midnight pranks than watch a Batman movie.

But I was also aware that he was a jealous and possessive person. He became angry easily. Life at home had been far from pleasant, but as children we had quickly adjusted to it. We knew when to shut up, and we knew when to keep out of the way of marital squabbles. Despite this trouble I had never suspected that the marriage was on the verge of breaking up.

With the first blow of the separation, my love-hate feelings for my father turned to pity. I really felt sorry for him, even though deep down I knew he had brought his pain on himself. When my brother and I visited him, he would probe us on what was happening. Questions like "Has your mother changed her mind?" or "When are you coming back?" were constantly fired at us. Soon I began to feel apprehensive whenever I visited him. I didn't like what was going on.

Slowly my feelings of pity turned to feelings of anger and resentment. He wanted my brother and me to come and stay with him. I suspected that this was his way of manipulating my mother, so I resisted. While I blamed her for initiating the divorce, I also knew she was only reacting to a painful situation. I knew how insecure she felt and how much she needed us boys to help her feel safe and not abandoned. Slowly I became aware of how my father was using us as pawns—quite unconsciously, I am sure. He would not deliberately have hurt us, but he was desperate; he felt his very survival was being threatened.

Feelings for God

My grandmother was a very devout Christian. During my early childhood her influence on me was profound. God was real to her, and somehow that was all the proof for the existence of God that I needed. She would read Scripture to us, pray, and sing hymns with us. And it was always happy singing; her faith was a joyful faith.

My grandparents lived about one hundred twenty miles from our home city in a small rural community. Their town is situated on the banks of a large river which attracts a lot of holiday activity. Large numbers of city people go there during the holiday season to camp, swim, sunbathe, boat, and explore the many islands of the river. My grandparents had moved there after my grandfather retired, and they were able to live off the small farm they established.

My brother and I spent every school holiday with my grandparents. We loved being on that farm! Not only was it a change from city life, but it was also a relief from the tensions of home. I always feared returning home after a stay with my grandparents, because I was never sure what I could expect. Would my parents be on speaking terms or not? Would there be fighting or not? Sometimes a return home would be happy. Most times it was miserable.

And so I learned to pray. Four or five days before we were due to go home after a stay with my grandparents, I would pray frequently. My prayer was simple: "Please God, make mommy and daddy happy." Sometimes it worked. Mostly it didn't. I considered talking to my grandmother about why prayer is sometimes answered and sometimes not, but I didn't want her to know how bad things were at home. So I said nothing.

Slowly my prayers changed from simple requests to outright demands. "God, you've got to make mommy and daddy happy." Then they became angry prayers. I argued with God. I threatened him. "Why don't you make them happy? What's wrong? Don't you love me?"

At about the time my mother told us she was separating from my father, I began to think that God was using my parents' fighting to punish me. The reason he wasn't answering my prayer was that I had been naughty, so I tried to find ways to atone for my sin. Everything I did or thought was carefully scrutinized to see whether I was displeasing God.

After the separation, I slowly came to realize that nothing was going to change. My mother was determined to get her freedom and start a new life for herself. A feeling of helplessness set in as I realized there was nothing I could do to change the situation or influence the outcome of the divorce. This resulted in a hopeless feeling, and I distinctly remember coming to the conclusion that the reason God wasn't answering my prayers was that God didn't exist. Or if he did he was too busy with other worlds or other parts of my world to care about me.

The Healing of My Emotions

It would be very sad if my experience of God had ended at this point. To be disillusioned with parents is bad enough; to feel abandoned by God is devastating. But that wasn't the end! I was too caught up in my pain to know it, but the slow process of healing was taking place even when I felt things were at their worst—and God was part of that healing.

I floundered in my emotional turmoil for about a year after my parents' divorce was final. Part of my distress was a consequence of the depression I felt in response to the loss of our family unit, but the subsequent disorganization of our family life also contributed to the problem. In the year following the divorce, we moved at least four times, searching for a living situation that was satisfactory. Everything seemed to go wrong, and my father was too angry and upset to help us much. I had to start a new school and make new friends.

When my mother announced her intention to remarry, my brother and I decided we would live with our father, at least for a while. This upset my mother, but she conceded to our request. I think she was too exhausted to put up any fight.

It was about this time that healing really began for me. (In retrospect, I can marvel at the resilience of the human spirit; it takes an awful lot of punishment to make any permanent dent in its armor.) There were three sources of help for my healing: my grandparents, my Sunday school teacher, and—believe it or not—my mother's new husband.

My grandparents were extremely loving and supportive to my brother and me during this period. If they were angry at my parents, they never showed or talked about it to us. They never interfered, except to invite us to visit them as often as we wanted. We slipped in a few weekend visits that were not a part of our regular visiting schedule, and those visits were like oases in the desert. They provided relief from the tensions at home and helped me to keep my perspective. There was always the reassurance that if things really got bad I could go and live with my grandparents. I even sneaked out one day while staying with them to check out the local high school. It was comforting to know that alternatives existed.

All through my childhood years I attended the Sunday school of our local church. While on the outside I would play the "tough guy" with all my friends (they didn't seem to go to church at all) and make out that I was only going to church because my parents forced me to, deep down I found church very satisfying. One teacher in particular impressed me greatly. She was the mother of another boy my age and served as the superintendent of our Sunday school. Earlier in her life she had contracted polio, so she walked with a limp. But what really impressed me was her ability to give love unconditionally. She never became irritated or angry at us, no matter what we did. She was a beautiful person all through.

She obviously knew about the breakup of our home, although she never embarrassed me over it or made it a big issue. But I could feel her love and concern; it was in her eyes and in the way she touched me—gentle but firm. Her message was very clear: there is more to life than raiment, and more to live for than parents.

Through this woman's influence, Matthew 6:33 became an important verse of scripture to me: ". . . Seek ye first the kingdom of God, and his righteousness; and all these things shall be added unto you." I came to know God personally, not for what he could do in saving our family, but for what he had done for me in dying on the cross. These words helped to free me from bitterness and hatred and moved me to the place of forgiveness for all the deep hurts and resentment I experienced. They helped me overcome the aftereffects of losing the most precious thing a child can have—his family. (When my wife and I became engaged years later, I had Matthew 6:33 inscribed on the inside of her engagement ring. It is still there twenty-six years later!)

When my mother remarried, I was too numb to feel anything. It seemed I had felt it all already; what more was there to experience? I did not meet my new stepfather until after the wedding, because my brother and I were living with my father at the time and it didn't seem appropriate that I should have contact with him. In the months that followed the wedding I occasionally encountered him, although I kept my distance. But this man simply accepted me for what I was and showered me with kindness. Although I was just thirteen years old, he treated me as an adult, showing respect for my opinions. He never put me down, and never insinuated that I was an intruder when I visited my mother. Slowly I came to trust him, and slowly my fears subsided. Imperceptibly, but very definitely, I began to see life return to normal again. New patterns emerged. Change was not an impossible mountain to climb.

My brother and I finally moved back to live with my mother when my father remarried and moved across the country. His life was also recovering, and my new stepmother turned out to be a real gem of a person. My mother had two more sons, and both my half-brothers are now a part of my life and my family.

I am now forty-nine years old—reasonably successful and quite happy. My marriage of twenty-six years is the pride of my life; my wife is a wonderful provision from God whom I cherish very deeply. My three daughters must be the best a father can hope for. But I often ask myself whether my life would have been happier if my parents had worked out their problems together? Even though my mother and father have built separate but happy lives for themselves since their divorce, I will always suspect that what has emerged is only a "second best."

2

The Damaging Effects of Divorce

DEBBIE WAS ALWAYS A CHEERFUL PERSON. Despite the fact that she was slightly underdeveloped for her age, she never brooded about it and could even laugh at the jokes her schoolmates would make about her training bra. But then one day she lost her cool.

"Get away from me—I hate you!" was all she would say to her friends. She would slip out of class before anyone could stop her for conversation. She became withdrawn and sullen.

"Is something bothering you, Debbie?" a teacher asked her one day. "Nothing's bothering me—I'm just sick of the world" was the only reply she would give.

Danny was quiet-spoken. As a high school senior he was popular with the girls, and while he didn't have a lot of self-confidence, he was successful at most of the activities he engaged in. He seemed to be set for a generous scholarship at a good college with the prospect of fulfilling a long-time dream of becoming a doctor.

Then one day he arrived at school to take a biology test. He sat down at his desk, pulled out a pencil from inside his coat pocket and twirled it between his fingers. The other kids worked energetically at the test, choosing the correct answers from the multiple options given; erasing the incorrect ones. Danny just sat there, twirling his pencil.

The teacher noticed this and asked him, "Is something bothering you Danny?"

Danny stood up from his desk and without a word of explanation walked out of the room. Two months later he was arrested for being drunk and disorderly.

These stories, and many like them, can be told all across the country. What do they have in common?

They are stories about the children of divorce, like my own story in the first chapter. These children have gone through one of life's most wrenching and painful experiences—the disintegration of their homes.

This is not a book about divorce. Rather, it is a book about the consequences of divorce on one party whose full rights are not always given adequate consideration. No sane parent deliberately wants to hurt his or her child. No responsible person would disagree that a child is entitled to fair treatment and reasonable consideration when a divorce is taking place. But in the emotionally chaotic atmosphere of a divorce, when each party is preoccupied with protecting himself and doing his utmost to minimize his own hurt, the needs and rights of a child can easily be overlooked. Not every parent is sane and responsible during a divorce. And this is as true for Christian parents as it is for non-Christians.

It Takes a Long Time to Get Over It

I can clearly remember the effect my parents' divorce had on my emotions. Because I was a boy, I would not allow myself to cry. When, in a moment of weakness, tears would begin to fall down my face, I would quickly wipe them away and make sure no one had seen me. Over the months and years ahead I developed a strong abhorrence for crying. I hated seeing injured animals or sad movies—anything that could make me feel like crying. Slowly I built a resistance to tears. I thought they were a sign of weakness, and I was determined they would never be a part of my life.

At first I only rejected crying in myself. Later I began to detest it in others. This made it difficult for my poor wife in the early years of our marriage. I couldn't stand for her to cry, so I would just "leave the scene" when tears came on.

As I began my career as a psychotherapist, I decided I would have to force myself to tolerate crying. After all, patients do cry a lot in a therapist's office; I've sometimes felt that I alone could provide enough business for the Kleenex industry to keep them making a handsome profit! So I learned how to put up with other people's tears, and even to be very empathetic with their pain. But I kept a very strict control over my own tears.

It wasn't until about eight years ago that I really came to terms with crying and learned how to do it myself. I began to see tears as a normal and natural expression of emotion. In retrospect, I can see that my freedom to cry only developed after my mother's death. Who knows, perhaps I had perpetuated a deep feeling of resentment towards her ever since she decided to divorce my father! Whatever the reason, now I can cry when I need to, and feel the freedom of this healthy emotional outlet. It took a long time to undo what I believe to be the consequence of a divorce at a critical stage of my life.

Don't Deny the Consequences of Divorce

Our world has its quota of soothsayers! These are people who want to protect themselves from the pain of others, so they go around reassuring everybody that everything will turn out fine. Since divorcing parents often—if not always—feel guilty about what they are doing, they gratefully accept the placating platitudes of friends who say, "The kids will get over it; it's amazing how resilient they are," or, "Divorce is not a catastrophe for children; they will survive it." This is not helpful.

While I do not want to create problems where none exist, I do believe it is time we more realistically evaluated the consequences of divorce on children. I do not want to increase anyone's guilt, but I do think it is important for parents and others to work at taking positive and constructive steps to reduce the damaging effects of divorce on children. I am convinced that my problem with crying would never have come about if either or both of my parents had taken the time to allow me a healthy outlet for my emotions. For me to have been able to cry with my mother and have her receive my pain with understanding probably would not have changed her course of action, but it could have lessened my subsequent problems with expressing emotion through tears. She, like so many of us, merely wanted to keep her own pain at a minimum by avoiding my pain. In the long run it made all our pain greater.

Some Children are Resilient

It is true that there are some children who can go through a divorce with little noticeable effect on their later life. They have strong, healthy egos, built by loving parents from the early days of their lives. They have adequate controls and psychological "safety valves" that enable them to release built-up tensions without becoming overwhelmed or immobilized. But it is a mistake to assume that resilient children are the ones who show no pain, or who act continually strong and courageous during or after the divorce! It is not necessarily a bad sign for children to cry a lot, or to act weak and upset. The immediate reaction to the announcement of a divorce can be very misleading.

It is safe to assume, whether a child seems resilient or not, emotionally healthy or not, that the divorce will have some damaging effect on him or her. This assumption will keep parents from being trapped into neglecting the positive steps that must be taken to ensure that the child's needs are being met. It will help if parents can avoid playing denial games about their children's pain. Just making this assumption should also free parents from feeling unnecessary guilt about the child. Admitting that there is likely to be a problem will free them from having to defend themselves, and let them get on with the job of helping the child.*

---

*If you have problems with guilt, I would refer you to chapter 8 of my book, *Feeling Free* (Old Tappan, N.J.: Fleming H. Revell, 1979).

Why Divorce Hurts Children

A prominent child psychologist, Dr. Lee Salk, has said: "The trauma of divorce is second only to death. Children sense a deep loss and feel they are suddenly vulnerable to forces beyond their control." This statement agrees completely with my experience as a clinical psychologist. Never again will most of the children of divorce ever have to face such a stressful period. The acute stress of shock, the intense fears, the feelings of uncertainty and insecurity, and the grieving over the loss of the traditional family structure will cause a child much misery.

Some of the more important reasons why divorce is damaging to children are:

—It signals the collapse of the family structure—the child feels alone and very frightened. The loneliness can be acute and long remembered.

—Parents have a diminished capacity to parent. They are pre-occupied with their own emotions and survival during the critical months (or years) of the divorce.

—The divorce creates conflicts of loyalty in the children. Whose side do they take? Often children feel pulled by love and loyalty in both directions.

—Uncertainty about the future causes deep-seated insecurity. Being dependent mainly on one parent creates a great deal of anxiety.

—The anger and resentment between the parents, which is so prevalent in most divorces, creates intense fear in the child. The younger the child, the more damaging this climate of anger can be.

—The children take upon themselves much anxiety over their parents. They worry intensely about their mother in particular, with the departure of the father (or the mother, in those rarer cases where it is the wife who leaves) being a terrifying event.

—If the family moves, a child may lose an at-home parent, a home, a school, neighborhood, church, and friends. Divorce represents a loss of so many things that a deep depression is almost unavoidable in children. Most parents fail to recognize this depression.

The Effect of Divorce on the Stages of Childhood

Pervasive as divorce is in our society, few children are prepared for it when it happens to their families. About 80 percent of the children receive no warning that a divorce is about to take place. Even when the news is broken gently, the reaction is always the same (and just as I personally experienced it when my parents divorced): shock, followed by depression, denial, anger, fear, lowered self-esteem, and a haunting obsession that they may have been responsible for their parents' problems.

But how do children of different ages respond?

(1) *Toddlers* (two to four years of age) often show signs of regression to an earlier stage of development. They become more dependent and passive, engaging in "babyish" behavior. Rather than feeding themselves, they demand that you feed them, and they revert to a need for diapers even though they may already be potty-trained. Some psychologists feel that the absence of the parent of the opposite sex at this stage may be detrimental to a child's sexual development.

(2) *Young children* (five to eight years of age) also regress. In addition, these children tend to take responsibility for the marriage breakup. They tend to have irrational fears of being abandoned and even of starving; these fears need to be confronted and appropriate assurances given. Loss of sleep, bedwetting, nail biting, a deep sense of sadness (often a masked depression) and a retreat into fantasy as a way of solving the family crisis, are all likely to occur at this age.

Some authorities believe that this age—when they are old enough to know what is going on but not old enough to have adequate skills for dealing with it—is the most critical age for children to experience divorce.

(3) *Older children* (nine to twelve years of age) experience anger as the dominant emotion. This anger is usually directed at

the parent believed to be the initiator of the breakup, but it is easily scapegoated outside of the family and directed at peers just at a time when the support of loving friends is most needed. Children may alienate those close to them—including teachers and close relatives.

The spiritual development of the child is most likely to be damaged at this age. Disappointment, disillusionment, and rejection of the parents' spiritual values could easily occur. "They are just hypocrites and I don't want to have anything to do with their religion" is a very common reaction.

(4) *Teenagers* (thirteen years of age and over) have a different set of problems to deal with. They tend not to assume the blame for the divorce as readily as younger children do; they have a better understanding of the reasons for the divorce. Nevertheless, they can also be deeply hurt and resent their parents for breaking up the home. They fear being separated from their friends, and as there is a natural tendency towards withdrawing and feeling depressed at this age, a divorce could accentuate these problems. It is common for them to isolate themselves and refuse to talk about what's bothering them.

Teenagers also feel the "loyalty dilemma" acutely. They know that mother doesn't want them to like their father (or vice versa). "How can you like someone who has done this terrible thing to me?" or "Don't you know what a terrible person he (or she) is?" is typical of parental attitudes that create conflicts for teenagers. Keeping the peace with both parents can be emotionally draining for them.

Which of the Sexes Suffers Most?

There is no doubt in the minds of many psychologists that boys are harder hit by divorce than girls. The reasons are not hard to discern.

Boys are taught in our culture not to show painful emotions: "Boys don't cry; boys have got to be MEN." Boys, therefore, tend to deny their negative emotions more than do girls; this denial can be the source of the emotional constrictiveness many men exhibit later in life.

More is also expected of boys. They are expected to be stronger, more resilient, more capable of taking care of themselves, but this is not necessarily the case. When their defenses break down, boys are often more devastated than girls are.

"Reconstituted" Families

Much attention is being given to stepfamilies, now referred to as "reconstituted" or "blended" families. Incorporating a new husband, wife, or "instant" brothers and sisters into a family through remarriage superimposes a whole new set of problems on the problems of divorce and family breakup.

Adjusting to life between two homes, often in reduced financial circumstances, is complicated and confusing enough for a child without the added intrusion of an unwanted stepparent. To make matters worse, a single parent—especially a mother— may not be in the right state of mind to make a wise choice about remarrying. For instance, the costs of litigation and maintaining two households can reduce a family's income enormously. A recent Census Bureau report revealed that only 25 percent of divorced, separated, or single mothers receive child support. So many single mothers rush into a second marriage merely to escape financial insecurity or diminished status. Under these conditions mistakes are made, and the risk of a second marriage disaster is very high.

Some Divorces are Worse Than Others

Of course, the nature, circumstances, and reasons for a divorce are important factors in determining how the people involved will interact during the post-divorce period, and also in determining whether or not the children will be able to mobilize their resources to cope with the family rupture. Not all divorces are equally damaging to children. Where a divorce is pursued impulsively or in anger, or where the divorce coincides with other unrelated family crises, the child's capacity to cope will be more seriously impaired. When parents claim to be Christian believers, the confusion and bewilderment that their child will feel over their failure to use spiritual resources can be devastating to that child's belief system.

The most damaged children of all are those involved in custody battles. Easily duped into switching loyalties, these children are swayed by appeals—often accompanied by ridiculous promises—from either parent. "You can have your own telephone," "I'll buy you a new bicycle," and "I'll give you a large allowance" are typical bribes used to win over children. In my experience, these struggles are seldom carried out in the child's best interest. They are nearly always an extension of the basic marriage conflict and engaged in as a way of punishing the other parent. Caught in the crossfire of such vindictive fighting, children can be scarred for life, and even the most skillful psychotherapy will not be effective in correcting the damage the divorce inflicts on them.

Most cases, of course, are not that severe. But children are hurt by divorce even under the "best" of circumstances, and many do not "bounce back" nearly as quickly as they are commonly presumed to do. As a matter of fact, studies show that, among children whose parents divorce, 37 percent are still depressed five years later.

Newsweek estimates that 45 percent of all children born in a given year will live with only one parent at some time before they are eighteen, and that twelve million children under the age of eighteen now have parents who are divorced. The report also says that around one million children a year suffer through the breakup of their families. Divorce therefore represents a life event that creates a formidable amount of unhappiness. It is a major problem for the church and the mental health professions in terms of sheer magnitude.

Can Divorce Be "Better for the Children"?

A common question that is raised is: "But can't divorce sometimes be a relief for the child?" Children don't think so! Less than 10 percent report being relieved by their parents' divorce—and those children who do feel relieved still seem to have difficulty adjusting to the divorce.

Far from being happy about their parents' divorce, most children—even those from troubled homes—seem willing to go to almost any lengths to get their divorced parents back together. In fact, cutting across all ages and both sexes is the common fantasy that somehow, somewhere, miraculously the parents will unite again. This fantasy develops as a way of alleviating the feelings of anxiety which are so prevalent among the children of divorce, and it may become the root of an obsession.

Such a fantasy is easily kept alive for many years; I can recall thinking, as late as ten years after my parents were divorced, "Wouldn't it be wonderful to have my children experience a united pair of grandparents, as I did when I was a child!" Sometimes fantasies of reuniting parents lead children to engage in bizarre behavior in order to bring about such reconciliation. One young child, whenever her divorced parents were together, would repeatedly take their hands and place them together. Another girl, a nine-year-old, would deliberately expose herself to the bitterly cold winter's air with hardly any clothes on, trying to get sick so her parents would have to take care of her—together. I knew one twelve-year-old boy who would pray that he would die so that his parents would each blame themselves for the catastrophe and feel so guilty they would reunite.

As children eventually learn, tactics such as these don't really solve anything. But they do shed some light on the question: Should an unhappily married couple abide by the old-fashioned wisdom of "remaining married for the good of the children" or follow the modern conventional wisdom that an unhappy couple might well divorce "for the good of the children"? I suppose that either rule, applied simplistically and without consideration of the complex nature of married life, can lead to disaster. And it is true that in marriages where there is continuous conflict and perhaps physical abuse, the damaging effects on children may be as serious as those divorce brings. On the whole, however, my experience as a psychotherapist and the research available to us on the outcome of divorce has led me to believe that, when it is at all possible, saving the existing marriage is infinitely preferable to divorcing; this course of action is far more likely to lead to a fulfilling and satisfying life for all the parties concerned. And this is quite apart from the theological implications of divorce a Christian couple must face!

Does Divorce Solve Anything?

People opt for divorce for complex reasons, and some of these reasons have little or nothing to do with marriage compatibility. Boredom, falling in love with somebody else, poor communication habits, irrational ideas about what one or the other partner wants from life, middle-age crises, and personal neuroses are probably more frequent reasons for a marriage breakup than is deep-seated, fundamental incompatibility. For this reason I believe that most marriages can be saved and turned into satisfying relationships, if both partners commit themselves to making the marriage work, and if both are willing to do some changing.

Unfortunately for us, however, in our culture we have long been the victims of seductive, romanticized notions about marriage. We have been duped into looking at marriage only on the level of a relationship in which certain needs we have (many of which are fantasized and irrational) must be met. When they are not met, our culture tells us, we have a right to end the marriage.

Premier among these distorted and fantasized needs are, of course, our sexual needs. Unfortunately our culture (and this includes our Christian subculture) has created a neurotic monster in sexual disguise; most married people are chasing a sexual satisfaction they mistakenly believe exists outside themselves. Disillusionment will be the result, because real satisfaction always lies within oneself.

In the contemporary view of marriage, commitment and sacrifice all too often have lost any meaning. In the process of losing these values, we have also lost the ability to achieve real contentment and deep happiness.

Contrary to what our culture has led us to believe, however, divorce is not the only answer to an unhappy marriage. I am convinced that the solution to most miserable marriages is to be found in creative counseling, sound marriage guidance, and, if necessary, individual therapy for the marriage partners—as well as in a mutual turning to God for help and healing. I do not buy the simplistic notion that divorce will solve these problems, because I have seen too many instances in which divorce created more problems than it solved—for the parents as well as for the children.

Research backs me up on this point. Of adults who are surveyed five years after their divorces, only about a quarter are resilient—managing to cope adequately with their new lives. Half are muddling along, just barely coping. And the final quarter are either failing to recover or looking back with intense longing to the time before their divorces, wishing the divorce had never taken place. Far from taking care of all their problems, for these people divorce has just added a whole set of new ones.

Are You Sure You Must Get Divorced?

Much of what I have written thus far is designed to cause Christian parents to reconsider their decision to divorce. I have deliberately avoided theological arguments against divorcing, not because I don't believe there are scriptural reasons, but because I believe the damaging consequences of divorce and the rights of children to live a life free of conflict and enforced readjustment to a split family are so obvious as to reinforce scriptural injunctions against divorce.

Nevertheless, divorce continues to split families at an alarming rate in Christian circles. The number of children involved in divorce has tripled in the last twenty years, and dealing with divorce is no less traumatic for children today than it was when I was a child.

If you are considering divorce, then, it is my hope you will seriously consider the following suggestions before taking any further steps to end your marriage:

(1) *Face again the scriptural commands against divorce.* Read Matthew 5:31–32, Matthew 19:3–9, Mark 10:2–12, Luke 16:18, Romans 7:1–3, and 1 Corinthians 7:10–17.

(2) *Seek another perspective on what is wrong with your mar-*

riage. Your pastor can refer you to a marriage counselor, psychologist, or psychiatrist, depending on the nature of the problem.

(3) *Be honest and willing to confront your own contribution to the problems in your marriage.* Seldom is a marriage problem caused by only one party.

(4) *Challenge the simplistic idea that "a divorce will solve all my problems."* Consider the consequences carefully and be skeptical of friends who push you to divorce, especially if they are also divorced. Often this is simply a way of getting you to join them and relieving their own guilt.

(5) *Accept the fact that all marriages have problems and that all relationships go through "seasons."* A "winter" now may mean a glorious "spring" when you have resolved some of your problems. You were in love once with your spouse. Why couldn't you believe it can happen again?

(6) *Above all, pray for patience, determination, wisdom and courage.* God will provide these to you. Claim what is yours!

(7) *Take the initiative, with the courage God gives you, to seek a solution to your marital problems.* Go to a counselor by yourself, if necessary. He or she will help you work out a way of involving your spouse.

(8) *Remember that love and hate are not opposites.* Love and hate always intermingle. Whomever you love, you also have a great capacity to hate.

(9) *Remember: all that it really takes to make a marriage work is commitment and a willingness to change!*

If your marriage can't be saved, or if you are already divorced, then I trust the chapters that follow will be of help as you seek to turn a potential disaster for yourself and your children into an experience which promotes growth and maturity. With a little effort, you can increase your children's ability to build a more solid, secure, and happy life for themselves.

3

Healing Your Resentment

HEALING ALWAYS BEGINS WITH YOURSELF. Before you, as a divorced parent, can start the healing process in your child, you must first begin to heal the hurts you yourself have suffered through your divorce.

This is not to say that healing is a once-only event. Healing is a process; it will take time to accomplish. Since it is a process, it must have a beginning and, thank God, it can be accelerated, even if it never has an end. All it takes is a little determination, some honesty with yourself, a measure of courage, and a strong conviction that it is imperative for you to resolve your hurt, hate, and need for revenge. You don't think you have any of these? Then you are a very unusual person. It is more likely that you are not confronting these feelings in yourself—either because you are afraid that they might get the better of you, or because you don't know what to do with them.

Who Hurts the Most?

In every divorce there are two parties who hurt: the one who initiates the divorce, and the one who is divorced. If there are children, of course, they are also deeply hurt; it is the purpose of this book to show ways to minimize this hurt. And there are usually others who are hurt: parents, friends, and colleagues. For our purposes in this chapter, however, I will focus on the first two parties involved—the man and woman who divorce.

Seldom is a divorce a truly mutual decision between the

spouses. On the surface both parties may appear to agree, but usually deep down one of them would prefer not to have a divorce take place. The one who initiates the divorce usually feels guilty; the one being divorced feels rejected. The feelings of guilt and rejection inevitably lead to resentment, which is a deep feeling of displeasure and indignation from a sense of being injured or offended.

It is my belief that the person being rejected usually feels the most hurt and is therefore the one who experiences the most resentment. But is this belief reliable and applicable to all circumstances? Is it not possible that the one doing the rejecting has been the recipient of years of hurt at the hand of the other spouse—hurt that is not obliterated by the relief of divorce?

The point I am making is that resentment is present in almost every divorce and can be assumed to exist to some degree in all the parties involved. This resentment must be healed before progress can be made in helping the children of divorce.

Why Resolve This Resentment?

It is vital to the well-being of the children of divorce, as well as to the parents, that all feelings of resentment be resolved as soon as possible after a divorce. (This is seldom accomplished before a divorce takes place, because the procedure of divorce is in itself traumatic for the people involved. I have known many marriage partners who appear to have it all together during the preliminary proceedings, but who go to pieces when the divorce becomes final!)

The reason it is so crucial for resentment to be resolved is that there will almost certainly be endless quarrels, coldness, arguments over money and visiting rights, and a strong need on the part of each partner to hurt the other. This places a very damaging strain on the children, especially since they are frequently used as the instruments of communication and hurt—the weapons of the warfare. And Christian parents are not free of this form of child abuse!

One Christian mother who was in therapy with me felt so

helpless in dealing with her ex-husband that she became obsessed with thoughts about how to turn her children against him. She would take every opportunity to tell them stories about his extramarital exploits and about how he would withhold much-needed money for their personal needs. Every dirty detail of their marriage was recounted to her children. When I confronted her with how damaging this could be to her children she exploded: "I will use my children against him! They must know what he's like. I want them to hate him!"

Divorced Christian parents are most open to sin when they are driven by the destructive power of resentment. This is why healing from resentment is a first priority for the Christian parent who is divorced.

Resentment—The Cancer of the Emotions

Resentment is not an emotion psychologists talk about much. I recently looked through the indexes of the dozen or so fairly new introductory psychology textbooks that line my bookshelf. (Publishers send these to professors quite often in the hope that the professors will adopt them as textbooks.) In none of these was I able to find any reference to resentment. In fact, I believe that outside the Christian gospel there is no real solution to the problem of resentment! This should become obvious as I proceed. Only the gospel of Christ is capable of healing human hurt at its very root.

I believe that resentment is the most destructive emotion that a person is capable of experiencing. Its damage is felt not only in the psyche, but also in the soul. It is as much a spiritual problem as it is a psychological one, and its solution lies in both the spiritual and the psychological realms.

The Way We Cling to Resentment

One of the brain mechanisms that keeps us sane is our ability to forget. I believe that God deliberately created us with a memory that fades. I know we complain about forgetting things at times, but forgetting is actually a great healer; it protects us from an overcrowded mind. If we didn't gradually forget some things (and think of how much happens to a person in just one day) we would go crazy. Our conscious storage capacity would very soon be all taken up.

The unfortunate thing about resentment is that it refuses to let the healing power of forgetting work. And when this happens, our hurts are kept alive for a long time. Our memories can recreate for us, day by day, the pain we have experienced, and this in turn creates a need to "get even," a strong desire for revenge.

I marvel at the ability of the human mind to carry resentment almost indefinitely. I don't see this capacity in my pet cat; he seems to forget injustices almost right away. But when we humans are hurt we don't forget easily. This is why, in Old Testament times, God set aside forty-eight cities in Israel which were to be used as "cities of refuge." To these cities, scattered throughout Israel, those who had committed involuntary manslaughter could flee to escape the wrath of the dead person's relatives and friends. (The "eye for an eye and tooth for a tooth" principle prevailed in their law, so even a person who unintentionally took another's life could be punished with death.) Those who escaped to one of the cities of refuge could remain there and be safe, but they could never leave again without fear of being punished.

Down through the ages people have retained the capacity to remember hurts for a long time. It seems as if resentment burns itself indelibly into brain tissue. Do you know how hard it is to persuade someone to give up resentment? As a psychotherapist I have tried many times and failed. People cling to resentment as if their very lives depended on it!

The Way We Justify Resentment

Most of us hold on to resentment by convincing ourselves that our resentment is justified. We say to ourselves: "I have a right to feel this way. See how much I have been hurt?"

If you are like most people, no doubt you can point to many instances in your life where you have been traumatized, either physically or emotionally, and can recount many times when you were criticized or your love was rejected. You could prepare a display of your hurt that would convince the most skeptical jury that you have been unjustly treated. And you would be right! We are all wronged at some times in our lives. But does justifying yourself help you get rid of your resentment? Does it heal your wounds? I have yet to encounter any evidence that harboring resentment makes a person happier or healthier. On the contrary, resentment tends to destroy the one who holds on to it— not the one who committed the original injustice!

If resentment is so self-destructive, then why do we cling so tenaciously to it? I believe that when we are hurting very deeply, we actually in some strange way enjoy our resentment. It feeds our self-pity; it makes us feel righteous. And it also feels comfortable. Nursing resentment and planning revenge are natural things to do; taking the steps toward healing resentment requires courage, determination, and a dependence on God's help.

The Way We Accumulate Resentments

Resentment has a way of perpetuating itself; resentment breeds resentment. One wife I know found that her husband was having an extramarital affair. When she confronted him with her discovery, he confessed the sordid business to her and asked for forgiveness.

For the first few months after the discovery and reconciliation, the wife seemed to be handling her feelings well. But gradually, and without even realizing it, she began to accumulate the memory of all the petty hurts her husband caused her. Every time he did something that upset her, she added it to the memory of his unfaithfulness. Eventually she became supersensitive, even paranoid. She couldn't trust her husband. She spied on him whenever she could, and even became suspicious about the way he dressed. "Why is he wearing that suit?" she would won-

der; "Why is he ten minutes late?" Resentment was breeding
resentment, and very soon she was unable to control her feelings. Eventually her resentment led to the breakup of her
marriage.

Another man felt he had been deeply harmed by his mother.
When he was a little boy she would keep barging into the bath-
room when he was there, to spy on him. When I met this man he
was in his late forties, and had become totally obsessed with
these hurts. His mother, now very old, was constantly the target
of his attacks. He would bring letters she had written years ago
into our therapy sessions, and he even made tape recordings of
conversations with her, to prove what a terrible person she was.
Nothing I read or heard surprised me. His mother was a kind
and gentle soul who was desperately trying to love her son. He
in turn twisted everything to justify and feed his resentment.

Does this seem like a rather extreme case of resentment gone
awry? Perhaps it is, but believe me, the picture it paints of the
power resentment has to destroy us is not exaggerated. Resentment can poison our lives—as well as the lives of those around
us.

How Should We Deal with Resentment?

God did not create us with a predisposition to self-destruc-
tion. As free-will beings we *choose* our own destiny, and if left to
ourselves we would certainly bring about our own destruction.
But God has not left us alone! He has provided a wonderful
solution to our predicament—in the gospel. As a psychologist I
continually marvel at how perfectly the gospel fits our needs
and provides answers to our problems, even though we don't
always recognize the help God offers us, and even though when
we do we don't always avail ourselves of it.

As I have reflected on God's healing provisions, especially in
the area of resentment, I have seen four important steps which
must be taken to defuse the destructive power of resentment: (1)
develop perspective on hurts, (2) dispose of the need for revenge,
(3) declare your courage to those who hurt you, and (4) deliberately turn resentment into kindness.

These steps are all consistent with a Christian perspective on hurt. Careful attention to them will provide healing for your resentment, and this in turn will make you more capable of helping your children overcome their own hurts. Adjusting to life after divorce is difficult enough for children. You as a divorced parent owe it to your children to provide the healthiest possible environment in which this adjustment can take place. As we examine each of these steps in turn, trust God to help you implement them in your life!

(1) *Develop perspective on your hurts.* If we could effectively and rapidly forget our hurts without forcing them into our unconscious, resentment would not be a problem. But we can't. Resentment does not allow our hurt memories to fade easily, so we must find another way to healing.

By "healing" I do not mean a magic erasing of our hurts! There are no shortcuts with God. It is helpful to remember that we always feel hurt in the present; it is not a carry-over from the past. If we are hurting now over something that happened last week, it is because our memories can still vividly recall the facts of the hurt. Healing occurs when our memories lose the ability to recreate the feeling of hurt from the facts of the past.

How do we accomplish this? One way is to learn to look at the hurts others cause us in the context of the hurt we cause God. To help us do this, Jesus told a very important parable, often referred to as the "parable of the unforgiving servant":

Then came Peter to him, and said, Lord, how oft shall my brother sin against me, and I forgive him? till seven times? Jesus saith unto him, I say not unto thee, Until seven times: but, Until seventy times seven. Therefore is the kingdom of heaven likened unto a certain king, which would take account of his servants. And when he had begun to reckon, one was brought unto him, which owed him ten thousand talents. But forasmuch as he had not to pay, his lord commanded him to be sold, and his wife, and children, and all that he had, and payment to be made. The servant therefore fell down, and worshipped him, saying, Lord, have patience with me, and I will pay thee all. Then the lord of that servant was moved with compassion, and loosed him, and forgave him the debt. But the same servant went out, and found one of his fellowservants, which owed him an hundred pence: and he laid hands on him, and took him by the throat, saying,

Pay me that thou owest. And his fellowservant fell down at his feet, and besought him, saying, Have patience with me, and I will pay thee all. And he would not: but went and cast him into prison, till he should pay the debt. So when his fellowservants saw what was done, they were very sorry, and came and told unto their lord all that was done. Then his lord, after that he had called him, said unto him, O thou wicked servant, I forgave thee all that debt, because thou desiredst me: Shouldest not thou also have had compassion on thy fellowservant, even as I had pity on thee? And his lord was wroth, and delivered him to the tormentors, till he should pay all that was due unto him. So likewise shall my heavenly Father do also unto you, if ye from your hearts forgive not every one his brother their trespasses (Matt. 18:21–35).

As you see, this parable was Jesus' response to a question Peter asked: "Lord, how often am I to forgive my brother if he wrongs me?" Peter's question was just another way of asking: "Lord, how long must I wait before I can get revenge for my hurts?" And the parable Jesus told is his answer to the problem of hurt and resentment. The key lesson is this: *No matter how much others have hurt you, your hurt is insignificant when compared to the hurt you cause God.*

Realizing this truth helps us put our hurts in proper perspective. When we understand that the greatest hurt someone can cause us is nothing when placed alongside the hurt we cause God because of our waywardness and sinfulness, the question of how often we must forgive those who hurt us becomes irrelevant. There is no end to how often we must forgive, because our debt to God is always greater than our debt to any other person—including our ex-spouses. When we have this perspective clear in our minds, we won't find it as easy to hold on to our resentment.

(2) *Dispose of the need for revenge.* It is natural that when we are hurt we want to hurt back. The origin for this tendency lies in our primitive need for self-preservation: "If you hurt me I'll hurt you, too."

In some situations this may be a healthy law, as for example when we are physically attacked. But when it comes to psychological hurts, the need to hurt back is not helpful. It becomes self-destructive because, instead of protecting you, it causes the other person to feel more hurt, and to try to hurt you again. Revenge on your part gives rise to counterrevenge, and there is no end to this cycle. This is how wars begin, and how individual lives are destroyed.

Let me illustrate what I have said thus far by telling the story of one client.

Susan, an intelligent and attractive woman in her mid-thirties, the mother of three children, discovered one day that her husband Bob was having an affair with her younger sister. She was outraged. Normally a rational and calm person, she suddenly discovered that she was capable of the most intense hatred. "I think I could even commit murder at this point," she told me, when, after realizing how much her emotions could control her, she sought professional help.

Susan's situation was of the worst kind. "If only Bob had had his affair with someone I didn't know, it would be easy to forgive him. But my own sister! I have to face her almost every day. I can never forgive her."

For a while Susan carried her hurt and resentment deep within her, concealed from everyone. She appeared to have forgiven Bob and her sister, but at night, while trying to go to sleep, she would ruminate about the affair. She fantasized coming in on her husband and sister and praying that God would destroy them both. She became irritable and angry at everyone. Slowly she became withdrawn and bitter. Her need for revenge now controlled her. "I think the only way I can rid myself of these feelings is to do something terrible to Bob and my sister" was her final, desperate conclusion.

To help Susan deal with her feelings of resentment, I first took her through step 1 of the process I have been describing. I reminded her of the parable of the unforgiving servant, and I asked her to see her hurt in the perspective of the hurt she had caused God. My task for her was this: With God's help she was to come to the place where she could clearly see and understand that her hurt, terrible though it was, was insignificant compared to the hurt God could rightly feel about her.

This task took a little while. Susan prayed hard about it, and we prayed about it together. But slowly the full meaning of this truth dawned on her. She was able to put her hurt in perspective. And she was ready for the next step—dealing with her strong desire for revenge.

I reminded her of the closing words of the parable as given in Matthew: "And so angry was the master that he condemned the man to torture until he should pay the debt in full. And that is how my heavenly father will deal with you, unless you each forgive your brother from your hearts" (Matt. 18:34–35, NEB).

How do we dispose of our need for revenge? By forgiving those who hurt us. THERE IS NO OTHER WAY! And what does it mean to forgive? Simply this: *Forgiving is surrendering your right to hurt back.* Of course you have a right to hurt those who hurt you; revenge is an age-old principle! But when you forgive, you give up this right. Why? Because *you* need to be protected from the hurt. Giving up your right to revenge is for *your* benefit, because if you give in to your urge for revenge there will be no end to the escalation of the conflict. God knows us all better than we know ourselves; that is why we are taught to forgive!

After many years of dealing with the problems of people in the area of anger and resentment, I am more convinced than ever before that the healing of our hurt memories lies in the giving of forgiveness. As we willingly give up our need to hurt back, we heal our memory of its power to hurt us.*

In Susan's case, taking the step from realizing how her hurts were paltry compared to the hurt she had caused God to giving up her "right to revenge" was easy, though it is not always so for everyone. When she gave up her need for revenge, she opened herself to a fresh experience of God's love, and found a new freedom from resentment. Susan was a free soul again.

(3) *Declare your courage to those who hurt you.* While forgiveness is always necessary when dealing with resentment, it may not be sufficient. Not everybody hurts you just once, apologizes,

---

*For further treatment on the topic of forgiveness, see my book, *Feeling Free.* Chapter 5, "Freedom from Anger," is especially relevant.

and asks for your forgiveness. Sometimes people go on hurting you! They may do it openly and maliciously, or they may do it unconsciously or inconspicuously, but in either case the pain continues for you.

What do you do in such a situation? Allow me to emphasize a point about forgiveness that is essential to healing resentment: *Since forgiveness is designed to protect us from our own anger, it is not necessary for our enemies to admit their guilt or ask for forgiveness.*

We give forgiveness, therefore, regardless of the attitude of the one who has hurt us. Having given forgiveness, we are then free to take the next step, which is courageously asking whoever is hurting us to stop doing it. To do this we will need to be lovingly assertive, honestly confrontative. We will need to risk revealing ourselves, which may even increase our immediate risk of further hurt. In the long run, however, we are always the better for taking this risk.

Let us suppose that your spouse is divorcing you. He (or she) declares he (she) no longer loves you and wants to start life over with someone else. To justify his (her) actions, he (she) drags up all your mistakes from the past or lists your many weaknesses and takes every opportunity to brainwash your children into believing that he (she) is good and you are bad, and that he (she) is doing the right thing.

Of course, your first responsibility is to move yourself to a place of forgiveness. Don't retaliate. Surrender your right to hurt back. Then you are free to declare your rights and insist that the hurting stop.

But first a caution!

The reason confrontation seldom works to bring healing is that it usually becomes a vehicle for punishment. It is used to attack or humiliate the other person, and this never accomplishes its intended purpose. Remember, forgiveness comes first! Then calmly, courageously, and assertively—without hostility or rancor—stand up for your right not to be hurt by others.

If you have problems in the area of assertiveness, I would suggest you read a book like *Beyond Assertiveness* by John Faul

and David Augsburger.* In the context of Christian love it will
help you be more honest and less defensive, to feel more in
control of yourself.

(4) *Deliberately turn resentment into kindness.* The healing of
your resentment is not complete without this final step. Psychologists strongly emphasize the importance of acting out your
beliefs to strengthen your beliefs. In other words, if you behave
as you would like to be, you can ultimately become what you
want to be. For instance, do you want to be a kinder person?
Then start behaving more kindly to others. You will find that
the kindness eventually becomes a part of your whole being.

St. Paul gives us this same prescription for entrenching our
healing from resentment. In Romans 12:17–21, he tells us never
to yield to revenge because in so doing we will be overcome by
evil. As an alternative he advises us to do the following: "Therefore if thine enemy hunger, feed him; if he thirst, give him drink:
for in so doing thou shalt heap coals of fire on his head" (v. 20).

St. Paul's words are merely an echo of what Jesus tells us to do
in Matthew 5:44: "But I say unto you, Love your enemies, bless
them that curse you, do good to them that hate you. . . ."

Now, most people's reaction to these words would be to say,
"No way!" We have difficulty with these ideas because we are so
preoccupied with the idea that those who hurt us are going to
get away without being punished. We want revenge. But the
gospel has taken away our right to punish. God says, in effect, "I
do the punishing around here; all I want you to do is forgive."

Do you want to know how to free yourself from anger and
resentment and obtain full advantage from forgiveness? Turn
your resentment into kindness. When we do this, what does it do
for us?

—It helps us put our money where our mouth is! If we say we
  forgive, we had better behave as if we have forgiven.
—It reinforces our belief system by giving us the feeling that
  we are in control.
—It protects us from our own anger and hostility.

---

*Waco, Tex.: Calibre Books, div. of Word Books, Publisher, 1980.

—It maximizes the chance that the one who has hurt us will not continue to do so.

—It keeps us from sinning, because our behavior connects with our attitudes.

—It places the blame for the conflict where it belongs. This is the meaning of the phrase, "for in so doing thou shalt heap coals of fire on his head." When we turn our resentment into kindness, we make sure that the coals of guilt and punishment are kept over the head of the original guilty party— because we keep our reaction from becoming a greater sin than the original act was.

Human beings are complex creatures. This is what makes us so remarkable and beautiful. But we can only become healthy and fully functioning when we obey the laws God has so intelligently created and communicated to us. The rest of this book will only be helpful if you as a divorced parent are in the process of resolving your hurts and giving up your resentment. With God's help you can do it. Believe this with all your mind. I've seen it happen!

4

Common Mistakes Made by Divorced Parents

No two divorces are exactly alike. Often what works to alleviate destructiveness in one situation doesn't work in another. But the destructive divorces I have seen have had certain characteristics in common—the parents have made certain mistakes that caused great pain for themselves and for their children. Some of these mistakes are discussed in this chapter because I believe that to know them helps to avoid them.

While no one is immune to making mistakes, divorce makes everyone especially vulnerable to certain pitfalls. Divorce is a highly charged emotional event that will test the best defenses and strongest character to the limit. You may be the most competent mother or business executive and have every aspect of your life outside your marriage under perfect control, but chances are divorce will bring out the worst in you and show up your weakest features.

Because of this, I would urge you to try to be totally honest with yourself and alert to the early signs of being out of control. Trust God to give you the wisdom to understand yourself so that you will not be lulled into believing that you are doing the right thing when in fact you are victimizing your children or destroying yourself.

Don't Condemn Yourself

Parents earnestly try to do the best they can for their children. When they find out that they have failed in some way, they usually condemn themselves for their failure, and thus intensify their own unhappiness and the misery of their children.

Since this chapter is designed to point out common pitfalls, it is bound to find you guilty in some respects. So at the outset let me appeal to you to use the discovery of your weak points as an impetus to growth, not as an occasion for self-condemnation. Failures are meant to help us grow. They are the "feedback" we need to show us where we have gone wrong and to point out the corrective steps we must take. When you fail, claim the forgiveness that God offers you for your human frailty. And determine that you will learn from your mistakes so that you can avoid them the next time.

Since no two people will react in the same way nor face the identical set of circumstances, there is a danger in trying to apply a set of principles to every situation. Be cautious as you evaluate where you are and weigh your unique problems. Seek help from a professional if you cannot make any strategy work.

Excessive Guilt

It is the unusual parent who does not feel guilty over a divorce. When either or both of the parents are Christians, the feeling of guilt may even be greater, since there will be a deep sense of having failed God through the divorce. It is important to point out here that there is a difference between *feeling* guilty and *being* guilty. You can both feel guilty and be guilty, but the two don't always go together. You can be guilty of some transgression without *feeling* guilty at all. On the other hand, you can feel guilty without actually being guilty. Most often, our guilt feelings are not in proportion to our actual guilt. The reason for this lies in our personality makeup.

Sometimes we can easily recognize when we are feeling guilty, but not always. Often, when counseling with a divorced parent, I have seen that he or she is totally unaware that there are underlying guilt feelings controlling his or her behavior. A typical conversation goes something like this:

Therapist: It seems to me you are feeling guilty about what you have done.

Client: I don't think so. I'm just worried about my children. This is the first time I have left them alone.

Therapist: But doesn't leaving them behind with your wife make you feel uncomfortable?

Client: Yes, but I've never thought of this as a feeling of guilt. Perhaps I don't really know what it means to feel guilty.

And the client then goes on to describe what he really is feeling—vague remorse, hand-wringing, excessive anxiety, and sleeplessness—but does not see these for what they are, namely, symptoms of his guilt feelings.

It is remarkable to me that despite our psychological sophistication, simple but subtle feelings of guilt are not easily recognized. This would not be a problem if it didn't sometimes cause damaging behaviors.

Controlled as we are by guilt in our culture, divorced parents will approach their children in a variety of ways to relieve their own guilt feelings. Parents will appease children, try to win them, cajole them, and yet be totally unaware that what they are really doing is trying to alleviate their own feelings of guilt. Discipline becomes a problem under these conditions, because parents are afraid to further hurt their children's feelings. As a consequence, many parents become depressed because they feel helpless and unable to deal with the problems confronting them.

One young mother I knew had left her husband and two small children because she felt she was being trapped by the cultural stereotype of being a mother and housewife. She wanted to be free "to be her own person." For months afterward (it finally stretched to years) she would regularly send her children small gifts just to "show them I love them." She refused to visit them, claiming a visit would upset them.

Despite the fact that she was a very intelligent person, this woman was unable to see how her guilt was controlling her. The small gifts were not for her children's benefit, but for her own. *She* felt better when she sent them. Not visiting her children was to protect *herself* from her guilt, not to protect them from the pain of seeing her.

The ways in which we try to reduce our guilt feelings are legion, and any of them may crop up in a divorce situation. One parent may become overgenerous and give in to a child's every request. Another may avoid responsibility or contact with his or her child—even moving to another part of the country to ease the feelings of guilt. Of course, all of these guilt-reducing tactics are both unfair and unfortunate for the child. They create confusion and distrust.

What to Do with Your Guilt: Some Suggestions

(1) *Try to understand in what ways you are susceptible to guilt feelings.* It is possible that you have an exaggerated reaction to blame, a possible hangover from a strict childhood.

(2) *Be more open in acknowledging your feelings of guilt.* Often our reluctance to own such feelings is due to fear that we will have to change what we are doing. This is not necessarily so. It is possible to feel guilty over so many minor and irrelevant things that we cannot allow our guilt feelings to control us. When we openly admit these feelings, we can then choose what to do with them.

(3) *Avoid playing games with yourself or others to relieve your guilt feelings.* Guilt needs to be dealt with directly. We need either to put right what is wrong, or to accept God's forgiveness for it—or both.

(4) *Make a clear distinction in your mind between being convicted by God and having guilt feelings.* It is easy to turn neurotic guilt into a god and thereby miss God's true prompting voice. Our consciences can't always be trusted. They are often controlled by forces tracing back to our early childhood and can be like some strict, overbearing, and rigid parent. People who are controlled by inappropriate guilt feelings find it hard to accept forgiveness, whereas those who are truly convicted by God respond readily to the forgiveness he provides. Learning to distinguish psychological guilt from God's promptings through our

conscience is an important task for all Christian people. There is no easy way to learn it—we each must discover it for ourselves.

The "Absent" Parent's Role Is Crucial

Often the "absent" parent in a divorce situation—the parent who does not live with the children—is not fully aware of how crucial his or her role in the post-divorce period is. Fathers, who are most frequently the absent parent, are especially prone to make the mistake of thinking it would be better if they kept out of the way. But while it cannot be categorically stated that a child who has contact with only one parent will inevitably be handicapped in his or her development, it is clear from research that those children who have the most contact with both parents are the least likely to be damaged by the divorce.

It is important that divorced parents make every effort to raise their children equally. Too often fathers abandon the parenting task to the mother even in intact families; this is tragic and should be resisted. But it is even more important that both divorced parents participate fully in the lives of their children. Living apart from the children does not mean that a parent should play a minor role in their upbringing.

Of course, if the absent parent is to be equally involved in raising the children, the parent with whom they live must make a special effort to resolve any feelings of hostility and alienation toward the former spouse so that he or she does not even in subtle ways prevent contact between the absent parent and the children. If there is severe conflict between the spouses, it is probably good to arrange things so that contact between the absent spouse and the children does not take place in the presence of the custodial parent. But contact there must be!

Sometimes it is argued by a well-meaning mother or father that the former spouse is totally unsuitable as a model for the children. While there may be rare instances in which this is true, I have generally found that it is not the case. Children need to know both their parents, even if one of those parents is not a good model. I have found that children are well able to make the choice themselves, and that they reject role models as unsuitable when they have to.

How an absent parent relates to his or her children is as important as the relationship itself. The most effective way is to share common experiences. Absent parents can go to church with their children on alternate Sundays, and establish common interests such as hobbies or sporting activities.

One father, during his marriage, hardly ever did anything with his two boys. The home conflict was so great he preferred to keep away on weekends or holidays. After his divorce he found a new freedom to be with his sons, but taking them to restaurants for meals—which was what visiting day had degenerated to—did not satisfy him. He decided to purchase a sailboat and learn how to sail so that he could teach the skill to his boys. This activity revolutionized their relationship. It provided a common point of interest, and over the years bonded father and sons like nothing else could.

Another father found that he could share an interest in stamp and coin collecting with his ten-year-old daughter. The young girl had started the hobby a year before the divorce, and the father, with the intention of building a better relationship, decided that he would also take an interest in it. The hobby eventually became as much of a passion for him as it was for his daughter. More importantly, it gave them a shared interest.

Finding common points of interest is not difficult; all it takes is commitment and a little ingenuity. The local library is full of ideas about hobbies and other fun activities parents and children can do together. (Incidentally, many *undivorced* mothers and fathers have also discovered that developing common interests with children is a way to become much more effective parents!)

Visitation Rights

More conflict arises over visitation rights than over any other aspect of a divorce except for money. The conflict may stem from inflexibility on the part of the custodial parent. Sometimes the visitation rights are used as manipulation to gain some advantage or to punish the ex-spouse. Whatever the reason, it is always the child who suffers from these conflicts. It is unfair to a child to allow this to happen; conflict over visitation rights creates tension and mars the quality of the visit.

Depriving the child of a visit to the other parent is sometimes used to punish the child. This is a poor choice of punishment because, while it may be very effective in the short run, it strikes at the root of the child's need for security and is destructive to his or her emotional health. Using such a punishment, therefore, is damaging for the child and self-defeating for the parent.

The visits of a child to his or her other parent should be treated with great respect. A host parent who has difficulty with this should seek professional help, because these visits are so crucial that nothing must interfere with them.

A very common mistake parents make concerning visitation is interrogating their children after a visit about the ex-spouse's affairs. Children despise this more than almost any aspect of divorce. One teenager expressed it this way:

> I hate it when my mother asks me questions about my father. I scream at her and tell her to stop it. It's the same with my father; it gets to the point where my father will tell me things and say, "don't tell your mother," and I don't like to lie, but when my mother asks me a straight-out question I have to lie. I'm not naturally going to tell her, and if I did my father would find out and get mad at me. It drives me crazy!

Another pair of teenagers (they are in fact twins) tell of a game they play with their mother. "Sometimes she'll get on our nerves and ask questions like 'Is your stepmother pregnant?' So I would say no while my sister said yes, then we'd switch and I'd say yes and my sister no. We'd keep this up till Mom got mad and stopped asking us."

Children also resent having to ask permission to see the other parent, or being asked to carry messages. The most common message is "Ask your father to give you the check," or "Ask your father why I haven't gotten the check." This forces the child to be the carrier of guilt messages to the other parent and sets up conflict between the child and parent. This may be the home parent's intention, or the home parent may be totally unaware of the damaging effects such a practice has on the child's relationship. Either way, such messages should not be sent through the children; these are issues parents should work out themselves.

Change Things Slowly

The longer I practice as a psychotherapist, the more convinced I become that people can tolerate slow change better than sudden change. When change takes place slowly, they can process it more easily and make the necessary adjustments more effectively.

When divorce is being contemplated, the rejected spouse has a tendency to interpret everything that's happening as catastrophic and to want to run away. "I'll sell everything and move to Alaska!" or "I'll go back to my home town!" are common reactions. Such response is due partly to panic and fear, but much of it is masochistic—it comes from a need to punish oneself so that one can indulge in self-pity.

Drastic responses and subsequent impulsive decisions can have a very unsettling effect on children; such actions greatly increase their already-high levels of anxiety.

When my mother decided to separate from my father, for instance, it wasn't really necessary for her to uproot my younger brother and me and to move us all to another part of the suburb in which we lived. The act of packing suitcases, leaving home and friends, and resettling in a temporary second home greatly increased the anxiety that I and my brother were experiencing. We were being called upon to make too many adjustments at one time. It would have been enough just to handle my mother's message that she wanted to get out of the marriage. I suppose she thought she was being protective of us, but it would have been less disturbing if she had simply sat down with us, explained what she wanted to do, and left us in our home where everything would have continued normally except for her absence while she and my father rationally discussed their conflict and planned a long-term strategy for dealing with us.

In essence, what I am saying is that stability and security are the best antidotes a child can have for the anxiety created by divorce. If at all possible, the child's home environment and regular routine should be maintained. This makes it easier for the child to adjust to the separation and divorce and minimizes the risk of starting an anxiety-related disorder which may take its toll later in the child's life.

Promises, Promises

An important rule for divorced or divorcing parents to remember is: *Don't make promises you can't keep.* Parents alleviate their guilt feelings about the divorce by making all sorts of promises to their children. Sometimes these promises are outrageous and there is no way they can be fulfilled. At other times they are petty, easily carried out, but because they were offered in order to relieve feelings of guilt the parent conveniently forgets about them when the guilt impulse has passed. This creates further tension between the parent and child.

One day, shortly after his divorce, Bob asked his oldest daughter, an attractive sixteen-year-old, "How would you like to go with me to Hawaii this summer?" She was thrilled. "Do you really mean that, Dad? Really?" "Sure," he replied, even though at that moment he knew he could not pay for such a trip. He was heavily into debt, his credit cards were fully spent, and, besides, he was not due for another vacation leave yet. Still, he made the promise, reiterated it, and set his daughter up for a major disappointment.

Why did he do it? To alleviate his guilt. He also knew that she had discovered he was having an affair with a work colleague and that this was what had precipitated his separation intentions. His intense feeling of guilt at that moment completely distorted reality for him. In a day or two he'll come to his senses, hope his daughter won't remember the promise, and probably try to avoid her for a while.

Peter was not quite as generous when he asked his twelve-year-old son what he would like as a "special" present. Peter's divorce had taken place just recently and he had an urge to be kind to his son. "Oh Dad, I want an electric guitar." "Sure, that's great. Let's go shopping for one over the weekend." The weekend came and went, and little Peter nagged, cajoled, and finally sulked his way to his bedroom. Dad was too busy this weekend; maybe next weekend he would have the time! But young Peter never got his guitar. Father never really intended getting it for him. The promise was just a convenient way of helping him to feel better. The fact that it made his son feel worse seemed to escape him.

In so many ways parents make promises they can't keep. Going places, doing things, buying things, changing things, are all promised by parents in moments of weakness to assuage guilt or to get the children off their backs. Such unfulfilled promises teach children that they cannot trust anyone, especially those closest to them. It is far better never to promise anything than to fail to keep a promise. If you don't promise something but then give it, the child has a bonus, and bonuses are better than disappointments any day!

This is one thing that is so wonderful about God. He never promises what he can't provide. We are told in 1 Kings 8:56 that "there hath not failed one word of all his good promise. . . ." A Christian parent, especially a divorced one, could do no better than to imitate God in this respect. A trustworthy parent will produce trustworthy children, even if their family is disrupted.

Forcing Choices

Feeling rejected by the ex-spouse, many divorced parents begin to feel insecure with their children, especially when those children are teenagers. Do they love me for what I am? Do they want to reject me also? These are the questions which unconsciously arise. To resolve this inner conflict parents may engage in a testing of the child's affection and allegiance.

"My mother asked me one day whether I wanted to stay with her or with my father," Betty explained to me. "'Why are you asking me this', I asked her. It's terrible when your parents do this to you. They get you to a point where you've got to choose between them. If you choose your mother, then you hurt your father's feelings. If you choose your father, then your mother is hurt. So I just say the normal thing—girls should be with their mothers, and boys with their fathers."

The conflict created within the child by being forced to choose can be damaging if it is repeated often or if the motive of the parent forcing the choice is to interfere with the other parent. Children are remarkably insightful and brutally just. They know most of the time what the parent is doing. They know if the parent is testing their love or using them to get at the other parent. Because they don't always feel the freedom to speak up against the parent, they may internalize their feelings, pull away, and build up resentment toward him or her for playing such games.

There is a host of subtle ways a parent can set up a child to make decisions that the child would rather not make. "Are you coming with me to visit Grandma, or are you going with your father?" "Do you want to go to church with me or with your mother?" "What are you going to do during your summer vacation?" Forced choices like these cause conflict for the child because they imply that if he chooses in favor of one parent, he will be rejecting the other.

If a decision has to be made, then the way it is presented can make all the difference. The choice should be stated in such a way that the child has the freedom to make the decision without fear of punishment or rejection by either parent. The following simple steps can help to accomplish this:

(1) *Admit to the child that having to choose between parents is a very painful task.*

(2) *Reassure the child that he or she has total freedom to make his or her own choice, that the child's choice will not affect your relationship.*

(3) *Clearly present the options to the child, making sure that you do not communicate any bias.*

(4) *Force yourself to accept the child's decision without resentment.*

(5) *Tell your child you are satisfied with the decision, even if it is against you.* This last step is important, because committing yourself with a positive statement like this can reinforce the feeling of satisfaction within yourself. Commit yourself to the way you want to feel, and you will be surprised how quickly you actually come to feel this way.

Discovering Yourself

A discussion of the many mistakes a parent can make in the post-divorce period could take up many books. The best help I can offer can be summarized as follows: *If you want to avoid making mistakes, come to understand yourself.* Humans can be remarkably naïve, and they often act with little self-awareness. We all tend to say and do things without knowing why.

With greater self-awareness comes the ability to choose whether to act or not. A parent who knows why he or she feels a certain way can avoid saying or doing something damaging. But a parent who speaks or acts without self-understanding runs a high risk of doing something wrong. It's like shooting a gun blindfolded; there's no way of telling where the bullet will end up.

Since for most people divorce is the result of accumulated failures, the post-divorce recovery period will only produce growth if a greater degree of self-understanding emerges after the divorce than existed before. In other words, a divorced person must benefit from the mistakes of the past. This can only happen if he or she takes the time to examine the mistakes made in the previous marriage and to extract from them everything they can teach about himself or herself.

Some of us can learn from our past mistakes. Others of us cannot—we need help. We need a sounding board, someone to talk to so that we can clarify our thinking and test our ideas. For this reason I strongly recommend that every parent seek some form of counseling or therapy immediately following a divorce. This does not have to be in a professional setting, although this is often the easiest and most convenient way to do it. A pastor, a close friend, or an adult group at your church can help tremendously.

At best, divorce is very difficult for a child to understand. To cope with the hurts and disappointments of a broken home, children need the support and help of two healthy, honest, and growing parents. As a divorced parent, you owe it to your children to be fully aware of what you are doing to yourself and to them. If the devastation of the divorce is turned in a positive direction, everyone will grow. There can emerge a closeness and depth of understanding that is often difficult to achieve in intact families. While I would not advocate divorce just so this can be achieved, there is no reason why one should not strive for it once divorce has taken place.

5

Your Child's Feelings

WHAT DOES A CHILD feel before, during, and after divorce? This basic question is very important, because the adjustments which must be made and the residual impact of the divorce on the child will largely be determined by these feelings. If you as a divorced parent can understand and accept these feelings, then find ways to help their expression, the detrimental effects of the divorce on your child can be greatly reduced.

God is the great comforter. The spiritual healing he offers to us in Christ can have a remarkable effect on the physical and psychological consequences of any traumatic experience. As a parent you have a responsibility to help your child receive that comfort and healing. To do this most effectively, you must first understand what your child is feeling.

Why We Run Away From Understanding

If a child is being affected very deeply by your divorce, it is quite natural that you will want to avoid confronting this pain. Why? Because dealing with the child's hurt makes your hurt greater.

It is only human to avoid the pain of others. This is one of the reasons many people don't like hospitals. They feel too deeply the pain of those who are sick; it's as if they take the pain of others upon themselves. This is what "sympathy" is all about, and it is a normal reaction. Those who enter the helping professions such as psychiatry, clinical psychology, or medicine, must find ways to overcome this sympathetic tendency or else they would quickly succumb to burn-out. In its place we learn to develop "empathy," which basically means that we enter into another's pain with understanding, but without necessarily going through it ourselves. By so doing we lose the fear of taking on another's pain and can more readily be of help.

For the parent, the sympathetic response is often aggravated by feelings of guilt. Parents blame themselves for what their children are experiencing, even though they may not be entirely to blame. When a child shows distress their first tendency will be to either run away from the pain, for fear it will increase their own, or to try to force the child—in subtle ways, of course—to stop hurting. This may be done by too much reassurance, by telling the child, "Pull yourself together, it's not the end of the world," or by other means.

Trying to stop a child from feeling emotional pain is *not* helpful. Pain doesn't go away; stopping a child from feeling only forces the pain into the background. And because it is not out in the open, this buried pain can do a lot of damage. It festers and poisons from deep within the psyche.

When a child is prevented from expressing his feelings, a very important process—that of grieving—is short-circuited. Whatever else divorce means to a child, it is at least a significant loss of the family unit. It's as if something has died. Much has been written in the past few years about allowing people who have been bereaved by death to experience their emotional pain openly, and about letting the grieving process run its course without being aborted or stifled. Why should the death of the family unit not cause the same grief and be given the same consideration?

In effect, I am saying it is important that divorced parents not run away from their children's pain nor try to take it away just so the parents can feel more comfortable. In so doing they will be better able to minister that comfort which God by his Spirit is able to give for the deepest of all human sorrows: ". . . comfort him [or her], lest perhaps such a one should be swallowed up with overmuch sorrow" (2 Cor. 2:7).

Comfort By Understanding

It is very clear from Scripture that not only are we to derive comfort from God; we are also to comfort one another (1 Thess. 5:11). To be a comforter, one must be an understander. The truth of this is borne out every day in the practice of a psychotherapist or counselor. People who jump in with words of advice without taking the time and trouble to understand how another is feeling are not effective as comforters—even when their advice is filled with the wisdom of Solomon. I would say that a thousand words of advice is equivalent to a few words of understanding. Why bother, then, with giving advice? Stick with understanding!

To understand a child's feelings about divorce takes courage on the part of the parents—courage to move into another person's hurts without fearing how their own hurts will be increased, courage to listen and even to take the blame without becoming defensive. But, paradoxically, parents who make the effort to understand and comfort their child usually find that they themselves are also comforted. I've seen this happen many times over.

I recently worked with a family going through a divorce. Of the two children involved, the older boy, who was fourteen years of age, had become deeply depressed. For many months, ever since he heard of the impending separation of his parents, his mood had been sad. He stopped working at school, so his grades dropped. He refused to associate with his friends, so they withdrew from him. He spent all his spare time lying on the floor in his bedroom, listening to music with his headphones so that he could shut out the world. His father, who was the main instigator of the family breakup, couldn't handle this. He, too, became severely depressed, and he pulled away from his son, feeling guilty yet utterly powerless to do anything to help.

"Can't you get my son out of his depression," the father challenged me during a therapy session one day. "No, I can't," I replied, "but you can." I then suggested that the father take his son on a fishing trip so as to give his son an opportunity to ventilate his feelings at his father. "But won't it make him worse?" asked the father. (What he was really asking was, "Won't it make it worse for me?") "Perhaps, but we must take the risk," was my reply.

The father agreed to try it, and that fishing trip was a healing experience for both father and son. They were able to really show each other how much they cared, and the father was able to develop a deep understanding of what his son was feeling. He did not defend or even explain his actions to his son; he just received his son's feelings. While this did not save the marriage it did greatly reduce the emotional damage the boy may have suffered. It also ensured that the deep anger and resentment the boy was feeling towards his father would not harm their subsequent relationship. The father's effort at understanding eventually brought healing.

What Feelings Does a Divorced Child Experience?

The feelings experienced by a child as a result of divorce will change as time passes. As in the grieving process following the death of a loved one, there are clearly identifiable emotional stages through which children pass as they try to deal with the divorce of their parents: (1) fear and anxiety, (2) abandonment and rejection, (3) aloneness and sadness, (4) frustration and anger, (5) rejection and resentment, and (6) reestablishment of trust.

These emotional stages are inevitable and normal. As a divorced parent, don't expect your child to miraculously bypass any of these stages. Pray rather that God will help him or her through them in a healthy way, and that going through them will be a positive rather than a negative learning experience. Pray for understanding, and for the courage to actively confront the stages of the grief process as you try to help your child through them.

In the following pages, we will look at each stage more closely, and examine what a parent can do to encourage adjustment at each stage.

Fear and Anxiety

The nature of the conflict between the parents just before a divorce can take many forms. In some homes the conflict is very visible; the yelling, screaming, and fighting send very clear messages to the children that there is a problem. But seldom do children, even in such a tumultuous home, expect a divorce to happen. Usually they deny the seriousness of conflict and engage in wishful thinking that all will work out in the long run.

At the other extreme, some families use the "silent" technique for expressing conflict. There is no fighting in front of the children, and no hint is given that anything is wrong. The children of these homes come to hate the long periods of silence between the parents, but they too seldom expect that any serious family breakup will occur.

So it seems that no matter how open or hidden the conflict is, the announcement of a separation and divorce is nearly always a surprise to the children. The first emotional reaction a child has is therefore one of fear and anxiety. (I link fear and anxiety together here, because it is very difficult to separate them, although for our purposes we could say that fear is a response to a real threat and anxiety is a response to an imagined threat.)

What causes these feelings? Suddenly a great unknown is opened up in front of the child and he or she is being pushed into it! Divorce is a threat to the child's very existence as he or she knows it, a shaking of everything stable and sure. It is an emotional earthquake of the highest magnitude.

It is natural that your child will feel fearful and anxious! Many of the classic signs of anxiety and fear may appear— sweating, restlessness, sleeplessness, nightmares, hyperventilation, tightness in the chest, gastrointestinal disturbances, and a variety of aches and pains. These symptoms are normal and they should be accepted as such, without overreacting or accusing the child of malingering. Give quiet reassurance and discuss your plans very clearly.

The important point to remember is that we all can deal with what we know far better than with what we imagine. If a child is not given the full facts, he or she is likely to think up even worse possibilities. The anxiety component of the fear will then become greater and will be more likely to have long-lasting neurotic effects. A child who knows exactly what is going to happen will more rapidly come to accept the inevitable—even if giving all the facts and being open with the child seems to create a greater negative reaction. In the long run, a child who knows what is going on will be better equipped to handle his or her fear than one who is left to wonder.

If a child is not old enough to be given all the facts—or if there are other reasons for withholding information—it is especially important to provide physical reassurance. Spend time with the child. Love him or her openly and frequently, for love is the great antidote for all anxiety: ". . . perfect love casteth out fear" (1 John 4:18).

Abandonment and Rejection

The reaction of fear and anxiety soon gives way to feelings of abandonment and rejection. Even though deep down they may know it is not true, the children of divorce often feel that they are being abandoned by the spouse who leaves. "If my father really loved me, he wouldn't be leaving Mommy and me," one puzzled eight-year-old girl said to me once.

Younger children tend to have these feelings more than older. They cannot distinguish between the parents' separating from each other and one of the parents' separating from them.

Sometimes the parent who initiates the divorce is already involved with or soon becomes attached to a second potential spouse. If there are children in the second relationship, the feelings of rejection can even become greater. Listen to the following story told by a twelve-year-old girl:

> My dad had just left home about three weeks when he told me that he was going to marry this other lady. Then he began to show me pictures of this other lady's children—a boy and a girl just a little younger than me. I suppose he thought I would be happy about this—me being an only child and all that, and feeling lonely a lot of times. Well

I began crying and shouting at him, right there in the restaurant. How could he do this to me? He never carried pictures of me in his wallet—or anything like that. It wasn't fair. He was leaving me for them.

Such feelings of abandonment can be significantly reduced if the departing parent can maintain a lot of contact with the child during the early stages of separation. This is usually the time when there is the most conflict between the parents and when there is likely to be little contact between the parent who leaves and the home situation. That means that an extra effort must be made to keep up the contact. It won't happen naturally! Telephone calls won't do it, either. What a child needs to overcome feelings of abandonment is actual physical presence.

In one situation where it was the mother who had left the home, I arranged for that mother to be at her thirteen-year-old daughter's home every morning for breakfast. The husband co-operated by leaving for work early enough to allow mother and daughter to be together for at least an hour before school started. The mother could see to her daughter's clothes, arrange the schedule for the day, and take care of other motherly chores this way. We continued this arrangement for three months, and then slowly reduced the number of mornings they spent together as other contact times were substituted. I believe this greatly reduced any feelings of abandonment the daughter might have had.

Aloneness and Sadness

Very early in the divorce process the feeling of being alone sets in. Things seem quieter, and children find they have more time on their hands. Regular family activities come to a stop. Meal times are no longer regular. Even the conflict that had become so familiar suddenly comes to a stop. There is less fussing all around.

When this happens, some children are surprised to find that for the first time in their lives they feel a deep sadness. It is felt with a pain in the stomach and a tightness in the chest. Hobbies become neglected. Pets are ignored. Energy is diminished. Eating is difficult, and most children lose interest in their school-work and friends. They just want to mope around.

At this stage children spend a lot of time thinking. Some of this thinking is wishful daydreaming, fantasizing that parents will get together again and all problems will go away. Some of the thinking only intensifies the sadness, and crying spells may result.

These crying spells should not be discouraged—and parents should avoid making their children feel ashamed or embarrassed for crying. Tears are an important outlet for the sadness children feel, and crying serves a very important physiological function in helping them overcome sadness and depression. It is characteristic of our culture that we tend to suppress painful feelings, to avoid crying, and I believe this has a direct relationship with the incidence of neuroticism. If we felt the freedom to cry more often, we would probably be healthier—both physically and psychologically. Perhaps this is what Jesus was suggesting when he said: ". . . Blessed are ye that weep now: for ye shall laugh" (Luke 6:21).

Frustration and Anger

Following close on the heels of sadness over the loss of the family unit comes the feeling of frustration. Children cannot get what they want—primarily security and happiness, and a return to the way things were before the divorce. Goals are blocked and needs are neglected. When this happens, children experience a deep frustration, out of which develop feelings of anger.

While anger as a response to frustration is primarily intended to help the individual overcome the source of frustration, the child caught up in divorce cannot achieve this end. Decisions are being made outside the realm of the child's influence, and no amount of anger on the child's part is going to change anything. The anger therefore becomes self-defeating, and is often turned inward by the child, who may do something to hurt himself. One fourteen-year-old boy in a family I was working with went to his father's workshop and cut himself quite deeply on the leg with a chisel. "I was just testing to see how sharp it was" was his excuse afterwards, but the depth of the cut and the deliberateness of the act clearly indicated that harming himself was the only way this boy could express his frustration and anger.

Since anger constitutes a major adjustment problem for children of divorce, I will be devoting a full chapter to a discussion of this topic. Suffice it for me to say at this point that feelings of anger must be accepted as a normal stage in the process of adjusting to the divorce. When parents overreact to these anger feelings, usually because they are feeling guilty about what they have done, they only aggravate the potential for more anger.

Children's anger should be received naturally, with the assurance that the parent understands why they feel the way they do and does not "blame" them for their anger. A statement like: "You have no right to be angry" doesn't help; children of divorce *do* have a right to be angry! What they need help with is how to handle their anger. "Tell me how angry you are" is an invitation to openness and a much better approach. A parent who can receive the child's anger without defending or excusing himself or herself will be helping the healing process.

Rejection and Resentment

Frustration and anger can give way to a period when the child rejects his parents. The child is not over the feelings of anger, but for now anger takes a back seat. The child may pull away and place some emotional distance between himself and his parent. This helps to protect him or her from further emotional pain, but may also be a way of punishing the parent for what has happened.

The rejection can take the form of pouting and giving parents the "silent treatment." The child won't come when called and won't respond when spoken to. When asked to do something, he or she resists or conveniently "forgets." Older children may become very critical and constantly complain about others—especially brothers and sisters. "That dress looks terrible," or "I don't like your hair" are common remarks from boys to their sisters and mothers. Girls may use a different approach, making unfavorable comparisons to get at their fathers; "Mary's father always takes her away at weekends," or "Sarah says her father never shouts at her" are ways of showing resentment.

We are all prone to say and do the very opposite of what we really want to say and do, especially when we are experiencing emotional pain. This phenomenon is known as "reaction formation." When we want to hate someone but we can't, we change the hate into love, which is more acceptable. This type of love may be superficial and have an "unreal" feeling about it, but sometimes it's the only way we can deal with our hate in an acceptable manner. In the same way, when we desperately want to be loved, but fear that we may be rejected, we turn our longing for love around and begin to show hate.

This is often what is happening when children go through the rejection and resentment stage. They push their parents away when they really want to be held, or they say hateful things when they want the parents to be loving. In this way they attempt to protect themselves from being rejected. In reality, of course, they set up a state of rejection, especially if the parent takes at face value what is being said or done!

One nine-year-old girl whose mother had left her husband would engage in this rejecting behavior. She would come into her mother's room and let go with a barrage of "I hate you, I hate you" statements. When the mother tried to reason with her, she would leave the room. The mother was confused and worried about her daughter's feelings. "If she hates me this much now, what will she feel when she is grown up?"

I reassured the mother and explained what reaction formation was all about. "Ignore the verbal statements and see the behavior as a desperate cry for your love and reassurance. Take her in your arms and hold her. If she fights and wants to pull away, keep holding her," was my advice. The next time this happened, the mother followed my suggestion. The child fought, screamed, and kicked, but the mother held her firmly and close to her, repeating the words, "I love you, Jennie."

Slowly the child quieted down and nestled into her mother's arms. She lay there still at first, but later began to respond and to return her mother's embrace. Mom had learned an important lesson: we don't always mean what we say, and often we say the opposite of what we mean. When she learned to listen for the real message behind the hate words, conflict was turned to loving.

Reestablishment of Trust

The final stage, in which trust is reestablished, is a very freeing one. When it happens, it is as if a fresh breeze has begun to blow in an otherwise hot and stuffy room. How long does it take from the beginning of a divorce until the final stage is reached? So many factors are involved that it is impossible to say. Recovery time depends on the nature of the marital conflict, on the age and personality of the children, and on how the parent has managed the subsequent problems. It could take a few months, or it may take a few years—sometimes it takes many years.

What can a parent do to make sure that the child's feelings return to normal as soon as possible? Giving attention to the following simple rules should help considerably:

(1) *Try not to be preoccupied with your own feelings.* It is so easy, during the difficult time of the separation and divorce, to be insensitive to the feelings of your children. Make time for their feelings. Set aside a period of the day or early evening when you can give attention to what they want to tell you. This will help you keep your own feelings in proper perspective and will give your children a chance to understand theirs.

(2) *Allow time for healing.* Divorce is not the time to be impulsive or to expect quick remedies. Your child needs time for important processing, so you will need to be patient. Ask God to increase your patience and understanding of what must take place before full healing can be expected. If this is a problem for you, then seek help from a pastoral counselor or other professional.

(3) *Maintain a stable environment.* Whenever possible, keep your children in their regular home, going to their regular

school, and playing with their regular friends. They have enough to adjust to as it is! Changes can be made at a later stage when everything else has become stabilized.

(4) *Don't become defensive.* Because you will no doubt be feeling very guilty about the divorce, you will have a strong need to defend yourself. This defensiveness invariably leads to more conflict. In particular, avoid attacking your ex-spouse for his or her actions. Doing so creates tension for your children, who have to keep the peace with both parents and should not be forced to take sides. Trust your children's sense of justice. They know, better than you, who is to blame and how much blame should be apportioned to each parent. Because you are a hurt party, you cannot be fair in your judgments. Leave these to God.

6

What Children Learn From Divorce

WHATEVER ELSE DIVORCE IS for a child, it is at least a major learning experience. And it isn't a single, short-lived experience either. It is an ongoing issue with which children must grapple for years. This one life-event can have far-reaching effects on the subsequent personality, attitudes, and abilities of the child to adjust satisfactorily to life. Most experts agree that it takes between three and four years for children to pull themselves together after a divorce. For an eight-year-old, this represents about a third of his or her life!

Throughout this period a divorced parent's behavior, feelings, and attitudes will be on full display. His or her true nature will be drawn out for all to observe. This would not be that serious if a parent's behavior did not affect anyone else. But since "modeling" is one of the major ways in which children learn *their* behavior, feelings, and attitudes, the consequences of the parent's behavior during such a time can be serious.

Modeling is the process by which one person imitates or copies another's behavior. It is a most important process in the development of a child's personality. This is one of the reasons our behavior so often closely resembles that of our parents. Without realizing it, we copy them from the time we are very small. The way they speak, walk, act, respond, and emote rubs off onto us. Much of what we pick up is good but some of it is of doubtful value.

Whether we like the idea or not, the conflicts surrounding a family breakup will provide important models for the children to imitate. To illustrate this, let me tell you of a woman who came to my office for therapy. Don't think of her story as uncommon; it happens more frequently than you realize.

Mary is the mother of a handsome seven-year-old son. On the whole, she appears to be happily married to a young business executive, who provides her with a very comfortable living. To all outward appearances this family should be happy, contented, and enjoying life—but it isn't.

When Mary first consulted me, she had great difficulty admitting what her real problem was. Finally, she admitted that she found herself hitting her son for the most trivial reasons—far in excess of what would be considered reasonable punishment for any misdeed. "Am I a child beater?" she kept asking me. She also had a tendency to use physical means to fight her husband whenever he angered her. "I have to leave the scene when Mary gets mad," he told me, "because once she starts hitting there is no stopping her."

Where and when did Mary learn this destructive behavior? As I explored her past, the reason become obvious—this was the way Mary's mother had dealt with her unsatisfactory marriage to a borderline alcoholic.

Often coming home late at night in a drunken stupor, Mary's father would so frustrate his wife that she would physically lash out at him. "Come and hit your father," she would invite her daughter. "He's a terrible man." At first Mary refused, turning away from the conflict, but when her father started retaliating and hitting the mother, Mary would lash out in childish rage, beating her fists on her father's chest in imitation of her mother and shouting, "Don't hit Mommy like that!"

Gradually, Mary had learned to deal with frustration by physically attacking the object causing the frustration. Now this behavior was coming out in her own marriage, which of course bore no resemblance to that of her parents. She had become the victim of unintentional modeling. The long road of therapy was used to teach her how to resolve frustration in healthier ways and how to stop using physical violence as an expression of her anger.

What Are You Most Likely to Teach Your Children?

Because conflict underlies most marriage breakups, the behaviors likely to be taught children during divorce will be variations of anger and hostility. When a marriage breakup involves little overt conflict, the atmosphere is usually healthier—that is, provided passive and indirect ways of showing anger are not being used to cover up deep hostility. Silence between a husband and wife doesn't always mean there is no conflict. Just because people are keeping their distance from each other doesn't mean they are at peace. Cover-up behaviors also teach negative lessons—such as using sulking and silence to handle conflict and manipulate people.

What is your child most likely to learn during and after a divorce? Allow me to mention a few traits:

(1) *Hate.* "It takes a lot more to hate somebody than it does to love them." These words were spoken by a thirteen-year-old girl, the victim of a recent divorce. She was referring to her feelings for her parents. But divorcing parents often give their children effective lessons in the energy-draining art of hate. And when they display their hatred for each other through vicious fighting, they teach their children not only how to hate, but the fact that hating pays dividends. Hating punishes people. Hate is a weapon more devastating than the sharpest sword or the most powerful bullet. When you've learned how to use hate, you don't need any other weapon.

(2) *Distrust.* Divorced kids learn that you cannot trust anyone—especially those who claim to love you the most. Simon is twelve. Listen as he explains, "We see my Dad every second weekend. When he picks us up (my younger brother and me), the first thing he tells us is, 'Don't say anything to your mother about my new apartment and things. It only upsets her.' As soon as we get home in the evening, Mom asks us lots and lots of questions about where we went and what went on, about his apartment and who was there and what did they say. I try not to tell her anything, but later she gets me to say something. I say to

her, 'Please Mom, don't tell Dad I told you anything!' Five minutes later I hear her shouting at my Dad on the telephone about what I said. I just know Dad's going to be angry at me next time." Later in life, Simon may generalize distrust of his parents to many other people; he may always be afraid to be open and honest.

(3) *Sneakiness.* Every divorced child I have ever met hates one aspect of what their parents want them to do more than any other—being called upon to spy.

A major task for children of divorce is remaining "friends" with both parents—and it's not that easy when each parent is trying to get the children on his or her side. The children often end up being unwilling "double agents."

Before her parents' divorce, one fourteen-year-old girl was recruited by her mother to check her father's car regularly for evidence of "another woman." "Search behind the seats, in the compartments, and in the trunk," she was instructed. Like so many others in her position, this little girl came to hate and despise herself for being so sneaky, especially when her parents claimed to be Christians and talked about "love and trust." She's lucky if she doesn't become sneaky and hypocritical herself.

(4) *Lying.* "If you are going to survive, you have got to learn how to lie," said one adolescent when describing the life lived between two homes and two sets of parents. "They lie to me all the time," he continued. "They used to lie about where they were going and what they were doing before the divorce. I knew my father was having an affair and so was my mother. When I called them on it they got very angry and said I didn't understand about these things. Now, when I go where I can get some fun and they ask me where I've been, I lie just like they do!"

These are all negative and destructive lessons. Are there not positive things a child can learn in a divorce situation? There certainly are, but it takes a little more effort and deliberate planning to teach them. This is true of many aspects of life.

Given the sinful and selfish nature of human existence, people learn the negative and destructive lessons of life without any effort. The positive and healthy aspects require a little more determination if they are going to be learned.

(1) *Love and kindness.* There is really no reason why parents who are divorcing need to engage in the hostile behaviors they typically do. Admittedly, the divorce is a most unfortunate end to the marriage, and one partner invariably does not want it to end. But should this be the cause of open warfare? If parents can get together and set aside their personal grievances for the sake of their children, they model love and kindness, even in the face of catastrophe, to those children. I am not speaking of love here as a feeling, but as behavior. I believe the 1 Corinthians 13 description of love is a prescription for how we should *behave*, not necessarily how we should feel. In my experience the feeling of love generally follows the behavior rather than preceding it.

(2) *Forgiveness for resentment.* While hate and resentment might be innate to humans, forgiveness is something we learn. A child who is not shown how to forgive grows up not knowing how. In a divorce situation, actions speak louder than words. A parent's every movement, attitude, and reaction will be observed by his or her children. For this reason, it is important for divorced or divorcing parents to do everything possible, even to the point of seeking outside help, to heal their resentment and practice forgiveness. Teaching forgiveness at a time when parents are hurting most must surely be the most effective way for them to teach it.

(3) *Patience and endurance.* Divorce is a time when decisions are made impulsively and when tolerance for frustration is at its lowest. It takes effort to overcome the frightening insecurities and the tendency to abandon hope. It is so much easier just to give up. At times such as these, parents can teach a powerful lesson about trusting God to give patience and endurance. If they do it effectively, their children will learn to do it, too. There is no better test for the validity of faith than at a time of trial such as divorce.

Improving Your Child's Resiliency

As I pointed out in an earlier chapter, children differ in their ability to bounce back after a traumatic experience like divorce. How can you as a divorced parent improve this resiliency? Obviously, whatever can be done to improve the way a child functions through this difficult time will also carry over into other areas of life. Even a divorce, therefore, can be turned into a force for growth. Here are some suggestions for making this happen:

(1) *Don't be afraid to be honest.* A child can cope much better with fears that are based on reality than with fears caused by imagination, even when reality is very much worse than what is being imagined. This is true simply because of the way we are made. Any threat to our well-being creates a reaction in our bodies that prepares us to deal with an emergency. In the case of reality-based fears, there is a limit to the threat. By contrast, fears based on imagination know no limits. The result is anxiety or worry, and we often turn little problems into big ones. Coping with anxiety and worry is much more damaging to both our mental and physical health than coping with actual problems, and the result is likely to be disturbances in the balance of our body chemistry.

Many of the so-called "psychosomatic" disorders have their origin in this form of anxiety and worry. Seldom do we develop these problems when we face an actual problem. God has created a wonderful body and mind for us, but we don't always know how to use them properly!

There are many reasons why parents fear being honest with their children. One is that they themselves fear the truth. Another is that they fear the way their children will react. But the problem with not being honest is that there is always bound to be a day of reckoning. Parents can only postpone the truth; they never change it! Their children will find out the truth sooner or later, and then they are likely to be more devastated because they will then realize they can't trust their parents.

Of course, being honest doesn't mean being insensitive. Timing is important; a parent shouldn't just dump all the truth on the child at once. In general, be guided by the principle that your child should not experience any unpleasant surprises or sudden revelations. Answer questions put to you honestly, and don't evade the truth unless you have very good reasons for doing so.

(2) *Communicate trust to your child.* Children want to be trusted. They want to be given responsibility, and they often respond with surprising maturity when they have been trusted. Children want to feel that their parents believe in them. I have yet to find a child who does not respond to trust. Often the most recalcitrant and disobedient children can be turned around by convincing them that they are trusted. Many therapeutic agencies dealing with juvenile delinquents are successful in their treatment because they use this principle. So don't be afraid to give responsibility. Allow your child to make important decisions or take on increased duties. He or she will thrive on this trust.

(3) *Give explanations, not defenses.* Because parents feel so guilty about what they have done to their children, they tend to become excessively defensive when giving information or explanations. This does not help their children. What children need are rational, nondefensive, clear explanations. "Just give me the facts, Mom," said one twelve-year-old boy. "I'll decide whether or not Dad is wrong." And he is correct! His mother was too preoccupied defending herself, and her son could see through it.

Why are explanations better than defenses? Defenses are too emotionally charged. The facts become distorted and therefore create further confusion in the child's mind. Explanations should just stay with the facts. They should be as free of emotional bias as possible. Objective explanations will encourage a child to come out of his or her corner and courageously face reality.

(4) *Give time for processing.* The human brain takes time to process things. When we are confronted with a major change in our life's status such as divorce brings, we need time to process

the change. The more severe the life event, the more time we need for processing it.

Parents often make the mistake of being too eager for their children to get over the divorce. Many forget that while they have had plenty of time to do their processing before they announced the divorce, the children have not had the time to adjust. Not allowing time for processing is likely to lead to impatience and increased tension, and will probably disturb the relationship between parents and children. When children are given time to process change, they bounce back very much more quickly.

(5) *Give freedom of choice.* One of the unfortunate by-products of divorce is that children lose their freedom of choice. They don't get to decide what happens to them; others do. For very young children this is not as critical as it is for older children and teenagers, who often feel violated because they don't have any say in the decisions that are made about them.

While a child's freedom to choose whether a divorce should take place or not is obviously restricted, there are many other areas where they can be given decision-making responsibility and a measure of control over their lives.

For example, whom should they live with after the divorce? What visiting rights should be allowed? Does the family move to another home? Should they change schools? Teenagers especially should be allowed to influence these important decisions and should always be consulted before the final choices are made. If they are party to the decision-making process they will not only feel better about the decision, but will cooperate more fully.

(6) *Build security.* A child's resiliency is greatest when he or she can bounce back into a stable and secure environment. This is why I advocate changing as little as necessary of the child's environment—home, school, neighborhood—during and immediately after a divorce. The more a child's world is changed, the greater will be the adjustments required. And the greater the adjustments demanded, the more likely it is that the child will not succeed in making them.

Dealing with Resiliency Failure

When a child is failing to adjust to the changes being demanded of him or her, a number of warning signs can be recognized. These will be the focus of the chapters to follow. At this point let me say that, if you are not satisfied with the adjustments your child is making (or not making), *seek help*. First, get as much information as you can. Ask the child's teacher for a report on how he or she is doing at school, and ask the other siblings how they see their brother or sister coping with the stress of change. Your minister or family physician can refer you to a specialist who can give you help with the problem.

Whatever the specific problem you may have to deal with, bear in mind that a divorced child usually has three questions on his or her mind: First, when will my Daddy (Mommy) come home? Second, when will my parents get back together again? Third, will they ever get divorced again? Satisfactory answers cannot always be given to these vexing questions. For many children there is no other way but to go forward accepting what has happened and learning how to live with their new life circumstances.

This year there will be over one million children asking these questions and learning that divorce is not just a bad dream that goes away when you wake up. To ensure that a child's processes of biological, social, and emotional growth continue in a normal and healthy way, it is important that parents be alert to the signs of trouble and have the courage to take corrective action before any serious harm is done.

7

Anxiety and the Divorced Child

IT WAS LATE ONE NIGHT when I received an urgent phone call from a former patient. Some time earlier, I had seen her over a period of four months concerning a personal problem. I guessed therefore that she was having trouble again with her husband. The problem in their marriage was not conflict and fighting, but indifference; her husband had lost interest in her some time ago and she had been forced to build an independent life for herself.

"My daughter is in a terrible state," she explained over the telephone, "I don't know what is happening to her. She needs help." She went on to update me on her life. She had recently decided to separate from her husband but had waited until a week ago to share her intentions with her two daughters. One was away at college, but the other, the subject of the telephone conversation, was still at home—a senior in high school. Two days previously, while preparing a project report for school, the younger daughter had begun sweating profusely, experiencing pains in her chest and difficulty in breathing. Most frightening of all, she had begun to feel the most intense feelings of impending doom. She was overcome by an intense fear and started crying so hysterically that her mother had to rush her to the emergency room of the local hospital.

After a day of diagnostic testing the message came back to the mother: There is nothing physically wrong with your daughter. She is experiencing a severe anxiety attack with hyperventilation. In other words, the daughter's anxiety was out of control and she needed to see a psychologist or psychiatrist.

I saw the daughter the next morning. She was still in a panic state and unable to tell me clearly what was causing her to be so anxious. Only after much prompting would she admit that there was any connection between her anxiety and the mother's intention to separate from her father.

Anxiety reactions before, during, or after a divorce are very common in the children of divorce. The reactions are not always as dramatic as that just described, but they are usually there nevertheless. For some children, anxiety reveals itself as regression to an earlier pattern of childish behavior such as bed-wetting. For others, it may be the start of a nervous habit such as nail-biting. Many adults who now bite their nails can trace the habit's origin to an episode, such as a family breakup early in their lives, that created a lot of anxiety for them.

What Is Anxiety?

Everyone is capable of anxiety. It is based on a fear-response mechanism that God designed into us as part of the elaborate system of self-defense that ensures the survival of the organism. If we did not experience fear, we would not live beyond the first few years of life. We would be destroyed by our carelessness.

Anxiety is a distorted form of fear. But not everyone recognizes or can accurately label the form of fear that we call anxiety. Some experience it only in its mildest form even during the most stressful of life's demands, while others feel it so intensely, even under very mild stress, that it totally incapacitates them.

Anxiety is a rather loosely used term for a vague feeling of uneasiness or fear. It is more than "worrying" and may be accompanied by many physical symptoms also. Occasional feelings of anxiety have no long-term damaging effects. When anxiety occurs over a prolonged period, however, or when it is very intense, it can give rise to many chronic illnesses. Many neurotic disorders can be traced to prolonged anxiety experienced in childhood. A child is rarely well-equipped to handle insecurity, threats of abandonment, financial and emotional deprivation, and the loss of a significant person such as a parent. Yet this is what every child must experience in divorce. Out of this experience comes anxiety, and if this anxiety is not resolved in a healthy manner, the child may have been launched on a journey down neurosis lane.

How can this be avoided? By recognizing the early signs of severe anxiety and taking a few basic steps to alleviate its causes.

How Divorce Produces Anxiety

There are many aspects to divorce that can generate anxiety as well as fear in children. I will discuss a few so that you may be better able to identify the causes and take steps to deal with them:

(1) *Feeling of abandonment.* As I have pointed out earlier, practically the first reaction of every child, especially the very young child who cannot yet understand the subtleties of adult relationships, is that the parent leaving the home has abandoned him or her. This creates an exaggerated need for the absent parent, much to the dismay of the parent who has stayed at home. "How can she keep crying for her father?" one distraught mother asked me once. "She's always ignored him before. Now suddenly he is everything to her." Such reversals of affection cause the home parent to feel rejected by the child.

While this is painful to the parent, the more serious problem is that the child may actually believe he or she has been abandoned. Many children cry out hysterically, "Why has Daddy left me? Why has Daddy left me?" Sometimes this feeling will lead to the child's thinking that he or she is the cause of the marriage breakup; such guilt feelings only increase the general level of anxiety.

(2) *Loss of a stable environment.* Closely related to the feeling of abandonment as a generator of anxiety is the trauma of losing a stable environment. Children need a steady, unchanging, and loving home base if they are going to learn how to be free from the problems of anxiety that haunt so many adults today. Neu-

rotic anxiety is most likely to occur in persons who do not have a stable home environment and who must carry a load of insecurity, hostility, and resentment dating from childhood. Divorce, of all life's experiences, has the greatest potential to provide this environment.

(3) *Separation-anxiety.* Some psychologists see divorce as an anxiety generator because it creates "separation-anxiety." When a child is exposed simultaneously to stress and isolation, his or her capacity to have a normal response to separation from significant others can be permanently affected. As an adult, such a person finds it intolerable when his or her spouse is absent or when there is a threat to their relationship. He or she constantly needs a protecting, parental person to take care of them.

(4) *Embarrassment and a sense of stigma.* Despite the fact that divorce has become commonplace and children know they are not alone in experiencing it, the feeling of being stigmatized and embarrassed is still a very powerful generator of anxiety. When my parents split, divorce was only just becoming socially acceptable. Even though my friends were understanding, and I knew that some were also the products of broken homes, I still felt intense embarrassment and anxiety about my home situation.

At the time of the divorce, I was repeatedly asked to explain the absence of my father. At school functions where I was participating in a play or sporting event, I would be asked, "How come your mother is here, but not your father?" Unthinking teachers, malicious friends, and unsuspecting strangers became my enemies; I was constantly on guard against such embarrassing questions. Finally I decided that it would be better if my mother did not come to school events, because then my father's absence would be less conspicuous.

When I attracted my first girlfriend, I was not quite prepared for the reaction that my parents' divorce would cause in me. I was barely fourteen when I became very friendly with a classmate. She was my ideal! She was also the class idol; it was a feather in my ego-cap that I became her special friend. I felt I had to be on my best behavior, so nothing would upset her. As our friendship developed (as best it can when one is fourteen) I began to dream about our future. Wouldn't it be perfect if we could marry one day? Then I sat up with a start! What will she think when she finds out my parents are divorced? She knew little about my family. I knew she had happy parents. What would they think of me?

I became depressed. Because of my exaggerated fears of her reaction, I decided to pull away rather than risk her or her parents' rejection. It would be many years before I let myself again risk the intimacy of another relationship with a girl.

As I have thought back on my fear of rejection, I have wondered whether my overreaction was due to being caught in an era when divorce was not yet as acceptable as it is today. But a few recent events have convinced me that such a reaction is just as common today. Many boys still feel this way, especially if they grow up in a Christian environment. One young man I know nearly called off his marriage recently when his parents divorced. The reason? The girl's parents told her that "children from divorced homes divorce more easily than others." Within our Christian circles particularly, there is still a stigma attached to divorce which can create anxiety and overreactions in children.

(5) *Fear of the unknown.* Perhaps the greatest anxiety generator of all is the fear of the unknown. The very young child is oblivious of what is happening. The older adolescent has begun to develop the resources needed to fend for himself or herself. But in between there are children who neither know what to expect nor yet have the resources to cope with whatever it is.

Divorce opens up a great unknown. It's like an earthquake opening a great crevasse in the earth. It is dark and dangerous ahead and a child is invited—no, forced—to go into its depths. What will happen? Will we be poor? Will Daddy give us a new Mommy? Who will she be? Fairytale stepmothers are always wicked. Will Mommy give us a new Daddy? Will he be cruel? Do we have to move? Where will we stay? What school will I go to? These questions and many others flood the mind of the child and create intense feelings of anxiety.

How Anxiety Shows Itself in Childhood

How can a parent know when a child is reacting with an unusually high level of anxiety? There are a number of important clues, but before discussing these let me emphasize that some anxiety (it is more likely to be mixed with fear) is normal and necessary to your child's healthy development. Let me dispel the idea that all anxiety is neurotic. The capacity to be fearful is a biological function necessary for survival. It is a warning signal drawing attention to a threat or something wrong in the environment.

Excessive anxiety, however, should prompt parental action. Anxiety disorders in childhood often begin as a problem focused on a specific situation such as the death of a parent or divorce. If the problem is not corrected early enough, however, the anxiety becomes entrenched as a lifestyle and is generalized to a wide variety of situations.

Jimmy, aged seven and an only child, had a severe anxiety reaction when his parents, without warning, decided to divorce. His anxiety showed itself almost immediately in a number of ways, but his parents were too preoccupied with their own problems to give him the attention and help he needed. After a little while, Jimmy's mother decided she couldn't handle his reactions and asked *her* mother to take care of Jimmy for a while. "He is playing up," she told Jimmy's grandmother. "I don't know why he is being so difficult. Just let me get over the problems I'm having with Bill and I'll be able to cope again."

Poor Jimmy now had a double trauma to contend with. Not only had his father left home, but now he felt abandoned by his mother also—even though she promised to visit him every second or third day. Unfortunately, feelings are always more powerful than facts.

In Jimmy's case the anxiety reaction which appeared shortly after his parents separated became considerably intensified. His mother finally reestablished a home for him five weeks later, but by then he had become attached to his grandmother and didn't trust his mother. Wrenching him away from his grandmother's home was a further traumatic blow. His original anxiety reaction to the separation of his parents slowly became a generalized reaction to all of life. He became an excessive worrier, fearful of many situations. He now spends an inordinate amount of time avoiding situations which bother him. His thinking is totally dominated by his problem. I know, because I am working with him now to help him find ways of reversing the influence of his early life experiences.

Divorcing parents owe it to their children to avoid creating such neurotic patterns. The child who is assisted in making the right adjustments by sensitive and nurturing parents, even though they are divorced, has a better chance for healthy adulthood than even a child from an intact but unhappy home.

The Symptoms of Childhood Anxiety

The symptoms of childhood anxiety can be divided into three kinds: physical, psychological, and social. I will discuss each of these in turn and illustrate them to help you determine whether or not your child has a problem. If it appears to you that your child has a serious problem, then seek professional help. Start with your pastor or family doctor, who will refer you to a reputable psychologist or psychiatrist. If your child appears only to have a moderate or mild anxiety problem, then try the strategies I suggest. If you see no improvement, then consult a professional. The psychological risks are far too great for you not to take positive action.

Physical Symptoms

Severe or prolonged anxiety can produce a disturbance of almost every system of the body. Children, like adults, sometimes have a "weak" system where they most readily show the anxiety. Some feel discomfort in the stomach or intestinal system, others in the cardiovascular system. Still others have problems with the respiratory system. Occasionally a child may show anxiety through symptoms involving more than one of these systems.

The most common physical reaction is in the gastrointestinal tract. Stomachaches, nausea, vomiting, or diarrhea can occur either continuously or sporadically. Often the child will only experience these symptoms when he or she anticipates some stressful situation, such as separating from a parent after a visit, returning to school after a vacation, or moving to another home.

Headaches are the next most common physical reaction to stress. Often a child will exaggerate the severity of the pain to get sympathy and attention. The most common type of headache is of the tension variety, but occasionally a true migraine headache may be triggered by the stress in a child's life. Migraine headaches are quite common among girls, especially after they have reached puberty. The migraine attack occurs shortly before the onset of menstruation and ceases before it is over. Differentiating tension headaches from migraine headaches is important because they are treated differently; a physician can be of help here. But removing the underlying cause— the anxiety and tension—is the most important aspect of treatment, and a parent can play an important role by providing reassurance, love, and understanding.

Cardiovascular symptoms are rare in younger children but can occur in older children, especially teenagers. Complaints of heart palpitations, cold hands and feet, chest pains, dizziness, and fainting spells are the most common anxiety reactions. The child may have a "hyperventilation" attack in which overbreathing triggers a host of strange sensations in the body.

Respiratory problems can occur at all ages. Increased frequency of asthmatic discomfort or allergy attacks, difficulty in breathing, tightness in the chest, and a greater susceptibility to chest infections can all be connected with anxiety.

Physical habits such as nail-biting, bed-wetting, and thumbsucking may either begin during a period of increased anxiety or, if these tendencies already exist, become intensified. Sleep may become disturbed, and the child may have more nightmares. Some children wake up at night screaming and come to the parent's bedroom seeking comfort and security; they may refuse to sleep by themselves and "act up" when bedtime arrives.

Psychological Symptoms

Increased irritability and a tendency to quarrel with other siblings and friends are common signs of anxiety. Children's tolerance for frustration, delays, and disappointments may drop dramatically; when they ask for something, they want it immediately. Temper tantrums may increase in frequency and be used by the child as an outlet for tensions and anxiety. I am sure you have personally experienced this tendency! You may be worried about something. The bothersome matter simmers on the back burner of your mind. Suddenly something you are doing goes wrong, or something you were hoping to get doesn't come, and you pop your lid! Your tantrum is out of all proportion to the trigger; the minor incident has simply opened the gate for your feelings, which all come gushing out whether they are appropriate or not! This often happens to children who are feeling anxious for one reason or another.

Children experiencing extreme anxiety reactions also tend to show disturbances of normal activities. They become clinging, and shadow their mother or father everywhere. These symptoms are directly related to the anxiety triggered by separation from one parent or the threat of further separation. They want to stay close to the remaining parent at all times.

Other anxiety symptoms are a morbid fear of certain toys and objects and a preoccupation with the fear that an accident or illness will befall their parents or themselves. Children worry about getting lost and not being reunited with their parents. Concern about dying may also emerge.

Social Symptoms

The first reaction a child may have when experiencing the anxiety of a divorce is to withdraw from normal social contacts. The reason for this is that the divorce triggers a grieving process which I will discuss in the chapter on depression. Another is that the anxiety saps the child's energy to the point that there is little left to devote to friendships and social contacts. Still another reason may be that friends ask questions which can be embarrassing and which do not have simple answers; rather than face the trials of explaining, the child prefers to be left alone.

The child may also become uncomfortable when traveling away from home or familiar areas, and may refuse to sleep at a friend's house, go on errands, or attend camp or school. These behaviors may be mild and can be treated with a little more pressure than usual for compliance. If the problem persists, however, or if the resistance is very great and the child stops all normal activities, a professional counselor or psychotherapist should be consulted.

Dealing with Your Child's Anxiety Problems

While it is most unfortunate when Christian parents must divorce, there is one major consolation in being a child of God: Our Heavenly Father does not abandon us when we have failed. He draws near, if we will let him, and offers strength and vitality, wisdom and prudence—"help in every time of trouble."

Divorced Christian parents, however, often feel abandoned by God. They say things like, "Why would God help me now when I have failed to keep his law?" or "I am sure God will punish me for not making my marriage work."

Nothing can be further from the truth! The feeling that God has abandoned you is always a satanic lie. It can be a by-product of your guilt and depression or even a result of extreme exhaustion. Before you can effectively help your child with his or her anxiety, or with any other problem, you as a parent need to restore your trust in God. Believe that he wants to help you deliver your children into adulthood free of the cumbersome problems that are created by divorce. Let your faith in him be restored. He will in no wise turn you away.

In developing a strategy for dealing with anxiety reactions, you should always remember that the root cause of the problem is insecurity—and I don't just mean physical or material insecurity. A child needs to feel emotionally secure. He or she needs to feel loved, not abandoned. A child requires a home environment that provides warmth and closeness, intimacy and openness, acceptance of humanness, and ready forgiveness for failure. These qualities in a home always produce emotionally healthy people. They should be the qualities that characterize every Christian home, but sadly this is not always so.

The belief that, if these qualities are not present in a home, a child will be better prepared or "toughened up" to face life more realistically is not true. It is a rationalization used by many parents who don't want to take the time to be better parents, or it may be a cover for their own neuroticism.

So whatever your child's specific anxiety problem, work at providing a more secure, emotionally stable climate for him or her. Give love and reassurance freely. Spend more time than you usually do with the child, and do not cut off your ex-spouse from contributing to this building of security. Your child needs to feel that both parents are continuing to stay in his or her life.

Turning now to more specific steps which can be taken to help relieve your child's anxiety, I would suggest the following:

(1) *Find out what is bothering your child.* Be an active and careful listener. Do not cut off the child, no matter how ridiculous his or her fears may seem. Listen to them to the point that your child can say that he or she *feels* listened to.

(2) *Evaluate your child's fears and be honest about which of these fears are legitimate.* You are not helping your child if you deny that a certain fear has any basis in reality when in fact it does. Lying or covering up teaches your child not to trust you. And, as I pointed out earlier, known threats are always easier to handle than fear of the unknown or problems that have been exaggerated by imagination. Anxiety is most often the product of imagined problems. When we know what we're facing, our internal resources are mobilized. We can then more easily take action, make decisions, or grin and bear the situation.

(3) *Give reassurance wherever it is needed.* You may need to give the reassurance over and over again for it to be effective. Irritably telling the child, "But I told you yesterday that we are not leaving this house. We'll go on living here" only provokes more insecurity by making the child feel belittled or put down. Patiently restate your assurance with words like, "Yes, as I told

you yesterday, we will continue to stay in our home. You have nothing to be afraid of." This communicates a quiet confidence which reassures the child. Slowly, if such reassurances are patiently repeated, the child will come to trust them.

(4) *Provide a stable and unchanging environment.* Again, the cardinal rule is: change as little as possible. Keep everything the same—except, of course, what is unavoidable—such as the departure of the one parent. To keep the environment stable, you may need to set aside your hurt feelings and ask your ex-spouse to cooperate for the sake of your child or children. More damage is done to children by the hurt and resentment between the spouses than is realized by most parents, so try keep these feelings under control and out of the picture when planning your child's welfare. If you can't control them, do not hesitate to seek divorce counseling!

(5) *Again, let me stress the importance of giving more time and attention to your child.* This is not always easy, especially when you are preoccupied with your own feelings. But make every effort to set your needs aside for the sake of your child. I suggest this, not because I don't think your needs are important, but because the danger at this stage is that you will become too introspective and self-pitying, and because these preoccupations are self-destructive as well as damaging to the child. Having someone else to take care of, someone to whom you can give comfort and attention, can help restore your perspective and "get you out of yourself."

(6) *Avoid communicating your own fears and anxieties to your children.* While, as a general rule, you should endeavor to be honest with your child about how you feel, it is important that you communicate your feelings in a way that does not scare your child. If you are experiencing a severe anxiety reaction to your divorce, there is a danger that you will communicate these feelings in a way that makes him or her anxious, too. Some parents make the mistake of sharing how they feel in too much intimate detail. They need to talk to someone, and since their child is conveniently available, they dump their emotions on the child. But this extra load of anxiety usually only intensifies the child's insecurities. Every person in the state of emotional tur-

moil created by a divorce needs to talk to someone. This sharing plays an important part in developing perspective on hurts, relieving tension, and restoring sanity by clearing the mind. But don't use your children for this. They are too hurt themselves to be effective counselors, so seek out a friend, pastor, or professional counselor to help resolve your own anxiety problems.

(7) *Provide acceptable outlets for your child's emotions.* Older children usually find it easy to talk about their fears. Younger children cannot always verbalize them, so provide them with games, paper and crayons, puppets, clay, and so on so they can express themselves. Do not criticize what they do. If they draw a picture of you as a devil, don't scold them; they are trying to express how they feel. Respond by saying, "Do you feel that I have been nasty to you? What is it I have done? What do you want me to do? Do you want to hurt me?" Asking questions like this can get children to express themselves in nondestructive ways. When they have expressed themselves, they will feel freer of the feelings.

But just because you release emotion today does not mean that you may not need to express it again tomorrow. Don't make the mistake, therefore, of expecting your child not to need the same outlet again many times over.

(8) *Respect your child's need for independence, even when he or she is searching for security.* If a child honestly wants to be left alone, leave him or her alone. Children differ greatly in their need to balance independence with security. They want you to be there, but not always in the room with them. Listen to what your child says and respect these needs. Do not withdraw your approval just because your child won't do it your way. A child's viewpoint is as valid for him or her as yours is for you. Accept these differences and go on loving your child in the same way God loves you—unconditionally.

Understanding Comes from Identifying

I have repeatedly stressed the importance of understanding what your child is feeling. Don't be afraid to expose yourself to these feelings. They are not "catching," unless you are already experiencing them yourself. The understanding that results is extremely important because out of it comes the right attitude as well as the right behavior. If you know what your child is feeling, you can better plan your actions and responses.

When parents come to me angry or hurt because they are baffled by their child's reactions or difficult behavior, I generally find that their confusion comes from failing to see the situation from the child's point of view. "He won't take out the trash, but sits there brooding" is the complaint about a sixteen-year-old, and when I talk to the son he explains, "It's the only way I can get them to understand what I'm saying, only they don't even hear me when I act up like this."

Each and every one of us needs to be understood from our point of view. Counselors are trained to do this; it is called "empathy." If parents could use just a little empathy with their children, a lot of pain could be avoided. A little bit of empathic understanding can literally revolutionize a home! Put yourself in your child's place. Imaginatively change places with your children for just an hour—or even a minute. Make an effort to feel what they are feeling, think what they are thinking, and experience what they are experiencing.

If divorced parents could dwell in imagination within their child's world and know intimately his or her concerns, fears, and understandings, feeling with him or her the experience of the divorce, I doubt whether they would have any problem knowing what to do. They would know what to do, because they would really understand what the problem is. Comprehending life from the child's point of view is the best training for a parent that anyone can devise. Doing so helps us to set aside judgment. It teaches us to understand the language of love, and makes clearer what it is we must do for our children.

When you think about it, this is exactly what God has done for us. He sent Jesus to live in the world with us and to experience our pain. Because of this he has earned the right to tell us what is wrong with our condition and to minister healing and comfort to us. Does anyone know us better than God or understand us more intimately than his Spirit? Jesus himself said, "But even the very hairs of your head are all numbered. Fear not therefore: Ye are of more value than many sparrows" (Luke 12:7).

Oh that we as parents could "number the hairs on the heads of our children." If we could have this degree of empathy and understanding for them, we could keep the damaging effects of divorce, as well as those of other life experiences, to a minimum. We might even be able to turn these things into maturing and clarifying experiences. We would be able to defend our children from all that would destroy them, especially the blows we deliver ourselves!

8

Anger and the Divorced Child

EVERY DIVORCED CHILD is likely to be an angry child. I say "every" because in my experience the circumstances surrounding the very few exceptions I have encountered are so unusual as to not be worthy of attention.

As I pointed out in an earlier chapter, very few children want their parents to divorce, no matter how much conflict is in the home. Older teenagers and adults may sometimes welcome their parents' divorce as an end to years of unhappiness, but in these instances the actual parenting stage has passed. In cases where one parent is totally destructive to his or her children because of a severe personality disorder, alcoholism, mental illness, or habitual lawbreaking, younger children might feel relief when a divorce happens, but even in these cases children usually feel a lot of ambivalence about the breakup. So whether the child wants the parents to stay together or not, a divorce is bound to cause him or her much frustration and hurt—a thwarting of life's purposes. And the invariable result is a state of anger.

Of course, this anger does not always show itself directly. My use of the term "anger" is therefore a broad one. I am using it in the clinical sense to denote the underlying, basic feeling that can be totally masked, suppressed, or hidden and not reveal itself in temper tantrums and screaming matches. Anger can lie dormant and only show itself through negativity and moodiness. But just because it doesn't show itself in a dramatic or obvious way doesn't mean it isn't doing any damage. These hidden and suppressed ways of showing anger, often referred to as "passive aggressive behaviors," can in the long run be more damaging than explosive, openly hostile behaviors. At least when the anger is openly expressed there is less chance that it will be stored up to explode in an unexpected manner, or turned inward in self-destructive ways.

As I will show, however, allowing anger to be openly and frequently expressed is also not the healthiest way to resolve it. This pattern, if repeated often, can breed an "angry personality"—someone who is consistently mad at everything and who believes that the rest of the world has been conveniently provided as a punching bag for his or her feelings.

No one who is angry has a right to take his anger out on someone else. The New Testament is very clear in its teaching on this point. Paul tells us, "If it be possible, as much as lieth in you, live peaceably with all men. Dearly beloved, avenge not yourselves . . ." (Rom. 12:18–19). Parents have a responsibility to teach their children how to effectively cope with their anger and how not to let it become a destructive force in their lives.

When Is Anger a Serious Problem?

Steven is twelve years of age. He has never been in any trouble, either at home or at school. He has always been a loving child, obedient, his pranks within normal limits—he occasionally would tie a can to the pet cat's tail or place stink bombs in his teenage sister's bath salts. But shortly after his parents separated, his pranks took a more serious turn. The family car's tires were found deflated one morning. On another occasion, when no one else was at home, he left the bathtub tap running while he went for a long bicycle ride. When his mother found the cat with its back legs tied together, she decided something was seriously wrong with Steven's behavior, so she sought professional help.

Mary is a child of seven. She is the youngest of five children and has always been a little aloof from the others. She resented getting "hand-me-downs," but never complained openly. "No one ever pays attention to me" was her regular complaint, but she never expressed it strongly, nor was she very demanding of her parents. She tended to keep to herself and compliantly did everything asked of her. And then one day her mother broke the news: Daddy won't be coming home anymore; he's found himself another wife and wants to live with her.

Mary couldn't understand it at first. Perhaps this was just a dream and Daddy would come back. But the days turned to weeks and, apart from an occasional quick visit, Daddy never did come home to live again. After a little while, Mary began to accuse her mother of "chasing Daddy away." She became disobedient when she was told to go to bed and would stay frozen in front of the T.V. When she was asked to pick up her clothes, she would throw more clothes on the floor. She did the opposite of everything asked of her.

Mary also started shouting at her mother, "You make me sick. You make everybody sick. That's why Daddy's gone away." The mother was at her wits' end. When she spanked Mary, Mary would passively receive the spanking, behaving as if she enjoyed it. Discipline lost its effectiveness, so Mary's mother, out of desperation, just left her alone.

When this happened, Mary's anger slowly subsided. With no one fighting her and perpetuating her hurt, she came to accept her father's departure as inevitable and finally reached out to her mother for love and reassurance. As a result of this, mother and daughter were drawn much closer together and found a new love for each other.

These two stories are examples of severe anger reactions in children of divorce. Both could have had disastrous consequences. In Mary's case a spontaneous and natural healing took place which did not need professional intervention. Steven, on the other hand, needed professional help.

When is an anger problem serious enough to warrant professional attention? There is no simple answer; experts disagree on the specifics of when help should be sought. Some believe, and I tend to agree, that in every divorce the reactions of the children need to be carefully reviewed by a trained counselor or psychotherapist. Parents cannot always trust their own assessment;

they have too strong a need to believe everything is OK. This doesn't mean that the children themselves should be taken to see a counselor, but at least one of the parents, if not both, should seek advice from a third party, an impartial person who can decide whether or not a problem exists.

As a general rule, I would say that if an anger reaction of the sort I will describe lasts for longer than four or five weeks, the problem is serious enough to warrant more expert attention than you can give. About 23 percent of those children experiencing divorce have a severe anger problem. Do not hesitate, therefore, to seek help if you are in doubt. Prevention is better than cure for problems resulting from unresolved anger.

Understanding Anger

To be able to assess the seriousness of your child's problem, you need to understand the nature of anger. Anger is the most confusing of all human emotions, especially to us as Christians. The ability to get angry is designed into us by God to serve a very important function, yet it has a tremendous potential for sin. Bringing these two aspects of anger together—its purpose and its potential for sin—is a major task for every Christian. I don't have space here to elaborate on this complex emotion.*
For our purposes, therefore, I simply want to point out that there are four causes of anger in all of us:

(1) *Instinctive protection.* Anger can be a reaction to feeling threatened or attacked—such as when our lives are endangered by a hoodlum or robber. Here the anger serves to protect us; it gives us the courage we need to perform some unusual task. Every policeman knows this type of anger. It keeps him alive, but it can also get him into trouble if it isn't kept in check!

(2) *Conditioned response.* Anger can also be an automatic response to a situation in which we have experienced anger before. We may have learned how to manipulate people by getting angry or how to get our way by throwing a temper tantrum.

---

*For further reading on anger, and the conflict it presents to Christians, see my book, *Feeling Free.*

(3) *Frustration*. Whenever we are frustrated, we get angry. This is a natural law; its intention is to help us overcome the cause of the frustration. But the trouble is that in many instances the obstacles are such that no amount of anger can remove them; they are beyond our control. By "frustration," of course, I mean anything that prevents us from getting our way. For children of divorce, this is perhaps the greatest source of anger. The divorce sets up many obstacles for them and removes many privileges. It blocks many dreams and demolishes many ideals. What can a child do in the face of these obstacles? The natural reaction is anger, but often the child doesn't know how to express that anger. This dilemma creates more conflict, more frustration, and consequently more anger. It is a vicious circle that seems not to have an end.

(4) *Hurt*. Anger is also a response to being hurt. The hurt can be physical, as when someone tramps on our toes and we want to lash out, or it can be psychological, as when someone criticizes us. Even when the hurt is psychological, there is a strong need to hurt back. If we can't hurt back right away, we store the anger up and wait for a chance to get revenge.

For the child whose parents are divorcing, any of these can be the cause of anger. Fear and insecurity can cause an instinctive need for self-protection and cause the child to lash out at the very ones on whom he depends for love and security. Patterns of learned anger response can trigger conditioned anger, and losing a stable home, friends, school, and financial privileges can set up many conflicts and frustrations. Finally the feeling that one or the other parent has abandoned the child can be the cause of much hurt. Because parents are often caught up in their own hurts, they can easily pass these on to their children without realizing it.

Anger as Protection

Whatever the cause, the anger triggered in the child, as in all of us, is intended to be protective. Anger is a warning signal, just like pain is a warning signal for disease; it alerts the person to the presence of conflict, hurt, or threat. God designed anger to be a system of defense.

Unfortunately, for most of us, life situations that trigger anger no longer need this protection. Anger was intended for a more primitive lifestyle, not the sophisticated, psychologically-oriented society of our modern Western culture. Many of the natural means of expressing anger—such as lashing out physically—are not acceptable in most situations. But the anger exists, nevertheless. It is an involuntary response to hurt and frustration.

It is important that the parents of an angry child understand this. Every child should, therefore, be allowed the freedom to feel angry, and be shown ways to express that anger without hurting others. Denying the child this freedom will only cause him or her to suppress the anger. There is then a greater risk that the child will use passive and indirect ways of expressing anger; this is always less healthy than being allowed to feel and express anger directly.

Passive Anger

What are some of the passive and indirect ways of expressing anger? The child may become very negative in outlook. Constant irritability, withdrawal and self-isolation, criticism of siblings or parents, and resistance to going to school or performing chores can all be signs of suppressed anger.

Some children may resort to more serious kinds of acting-out behaviors—even antisocial or criminal activity—to express anger. One fifteen-year-old boy I worked with developed a compulsion to damage other people's automobiles. When walking down the street in the evening, he could not resist the impulse to deflate tires or scratch the paint with a nail. His internal, but unrecognized, rage was so great he felt he had to do damage to something. What was causing this rage and why was he focusing it on automobiles? As you can guess, his parents had recently divorced after his father had left his mother for another woman, and his father loved automobiles! They were the pride of his life!

Even in this case, the feelings of anger the boy was feeling

were natural and appropriate. What was wrong was *how* the
boy expressed his anger. He should have been taught by his
parents at a much earlier age to recognize his anger and talk
about it with the person causing it. This is precisely what therapy did for him. It helped him to openly admit his anger and find
an outlet for it through talking. Shortly after he started therapy
his compulsive behaviors stopped.

How Much Expression of Anger Should Be Encouraged?

The question facing every parent and counselor in dealing
with an anger problem is how much expression of the anger
should be allowed? Should a child be encouraged to give vent to
every angry impulse?

To answer this question it is important to distinguish between
anger as feeling or emotion and anger as behavior or aggression.
The *feeling* of anger should never be inhibited. One should always have the freedom to feel one's anger. In fact, the more open
we are in admitting when we feel angry, the better. Being in
touch with the feeling of anger helps us to recognize that something is bothering us. It signals that we are being threatened or
hurt. If we accept the anger feeling and then try to discover what
is causing it, we can then take steps to deal with the cause.

But the feeling of anger also creates in us an impulse to behave in a certain way. We want to attack the cause or repay the
hurt we've experienced. This aggressive behavior is what gets us
into trouble. To feel our anger is healthy. To express it in hostility or violence is not always healthy. This is why Paul says to us
in Ephesians 4:26: "Be ye angry, and sin not: let not the sun go
down upon your wrath." The New English Bible translates this
as "If you are angry, do not let anger lead you into sin. . . ." My
understanding of what Paul is saying is that it is not anger itself
(as feeling) that is the problem, but the fact that anger has the
potential (in behavior) to lead us into sin.

In dealing with an angry child, therefore, a parent needs to
remember this distinction. It is important to help a child recog-

nize and talk about his feelings of anger—at the same time making it clear that certain kinds of angry behavior are not acceptable. A child should be able to say, "I feel angry. I hate you for what you have done" without the parent becoming upset or feeling defensive. This, of course, is not easy for divorced parents, who usually feel very guilty for what has been done to the child, and whose guilt is usually intensified by any expression of the child's emotional pain. Parents must make a deliberate effort to set aside their own pain if they are going to allow their children a freer expression of anger.

The Father's Role in Dealing with Anger Problems

One of the important findings of recent research is that children are more likely to feel anger towards the divorcing father than toward the mother, and that anger problems are more likely to be present in boys than in girls. I suspect this is because we raise boys in our culture differently than girls, and because it is more customary for fathers to leave home than mothers. Whatever the reason, this evidence does show how very important it is for the father to participate in healing a child's anger. An absent father, or a father who has difficulty in dealing with emotion, is going to aggravate the problem further.

It is unfortunate that our culture teaches males to hide emotion. Men, as a rule, don't feel as comfortable with emotional matters as women do. This is why so many more women are willing to seek therapy than men. It's not because women are more neurotic, but because they tend to be more honest about themselves and their feelings. I believe that men, because of their tendency to conceal their emotions, are generally more neurotic. They are certainly more difficult to do therapy with.

Of course, there are also women who have difficulty dealing with emotions, just as there are men who feel comfortable with their feelings. And girls as well as boys can display anger problems. The following list of ways fathers can help their sons overcome anger problems could of course also apply to mothers and daughters who struggle with expressing feelings of anger.

(1) *Be available.* Spend time with your child. Once a week is not enough. Two or three times a week is better.

(2) *Be alone with your problem child.* If more than one child is involved, spend some time with each child separately.

(3) *Work at becoming a better listener.* Men tend to be advice givers. Ask questions that encourage your child to talk about his or her feelings of anger, and try to receive these feelings without defending yourself. The more this happens, the quicker the anger will be resolved.

(4) *Watch for indirect signs of anger.* Consistent teasing, tattling, sarcasm, negativity, and resistance are common. Sometimes the anger will reveal itself through physical complaints such as stomachaches, asthma, vomiting, and sleeplessness.

(5) *Accept the anger as normal, but encourage the child to talk about it instead of acting it out.* Never encourage your child to take his or her anger out physically by hitting you or any other person or object. Anger can be resolved by talking about it; it does *not* need to be given behavioral expression through aggression. Vigorous exercise such as running or bicycling may help some children vent their frustrations harmlessly, but such exercise should never be a substitute for talking through those feelings.

(6) *Model through your own behavior how to deal with anger.* Tell the child how you feel, but do not "dump" your feelings on him or her. Try to show the child how to be honest with his or her feelings without aggressively acting them out. Such modeling, especially from a father to a son, can be worth many words. A child should see that adults can talk about feelings such as anger openly and honestly also, and not just expect children to do it.

9

Improving Your Child's Self-Esteem

Divorce is never a pleasant experience, even when the spouses mutually agree on the ending of a marriage. When the breakup is full of resentment and bitterness, the consequences are potentially more damaging. A damaging aspect of any divorce is the devastating blow it deals to the way the people involved value themselves—to their self-esteem. This is true for all parties, but especially for the children, whose self-concepts are still in the process of being formed. For them, divorce starts a chain of events that, if unchecked, can leave permanent scars on their self-esteem.

The damage to a child's self-esteem during a divorce usually comes not so much from the loss of united parents and a single home as from the indignities caused by other people's reactions, the legal process, and the way the child is battered emotionally. When children are treated like pieces of property to be bartered, when their feelings and wishes are ignored, when they are used as hostages in a parent's effort to gain material advantages in a settlement, or when they are used as weapons to satisfy an urge for revenge against the other spouse, you have a situation that has the potential to do a great deal of harm to the way a child values himself or herself. Such behaviors should clearly not characterize Christian believers. They violate every principle of love taught to us in the New Testament. And yet there are many Christian parents guilty of these reactions. I can only assume this is because they are acting out of ignorance. When they are better informed these behaviors are changed.

108

The Christian and Self-Esteem

There is a lot of confusion in the minds of many Christians about the appropriateness of the self-esteem concept. Much of the confusion arises because the psychological concept of self-worth is not clearly understood and the biblical teaching on the basic sinfulness of the human person is seen to be in contradiction to it. It is true that Scripture teaches us not to be self-seeking. We are called to a life of sacrifice and consideration for others. But none of these teachings is in opposition to the need every person has to feel valued and to have self-respect. In fact, claiming to have received God's forgiveness and yet continuing to feel no self-respect or self-esteem is a contradiction. If God loves us enough to forgive us, who are we not to forgive and love ourselves?

It is true that there is a form of "self-love" that is not acceptable to us as Christians. It is a type of self-worship that places ourselves above others (even God) and causes us to selfishly pursue our own needs regardless of how doing so affects others. This form of self-worship—I don't like to call it self-love because it actually has nothing to do with love—is not the same as self-esteem. In fact, it is really an exaggerated compensation for very deep feelings of low self-worth.

What then is self-esteem? It is how a person feels about himself. Each of us has a "self-image," a picture in our mind's eye of who and what we are. This image is formed early in our lives, and our parents play a major role in establishing it. As we grow up, we place a value on ourselves—either we are good, or bad, or somewhere in-between. This overall judgment of ourselves is what we call "self-esteem." When we say a person has a high self-esteem, we mean that he or she has a strong sense of self-respect and feeling of self-worth. By low self-esteem we mean that a person does not place much value on himself or herself. I call low self-esteem "self-hate," and strongly believe that Christian believers must not perpetuate such a feeling. God cannot fully express himself through vessels that do not value themselves.

It is also important to understand the difference between conceit and self-esteem. Conceit is a whitewash to cover low self-esteem. When we are conceited, our self-image is distorted. We tell ourselves we are better than we are, because in reality we cannot accept ourselves. But when our self-esteem is high, we don't waste time and energy trying to prove we are somebody. We don't criticize or judge others so we can feel better. There is a quiet acceptance of who we are and a deep sense of assurance that this is acceptable. Since God has made us his heirs, why should we go on believing we are valueless?

A Christian Approach to Self-Esteem

My understanding of New Testament teaching is that self-esteem is the same as the self-love of which Jesus speaks in Mark 12:31: "And . . . thou shalt love thy neighbor as thyself." While the primary emphasis Jesus is giving here is on loving our neighbors, he does not say that we must not love ourselves. He assumes that we already do this!

I think that the direct expression of problems with low self-esteem were almost unknown in New Testament times. In Africa, where I have had contact with many Zulu people, low self-esteem is also extremely rare. Zulu men and women derive self-esteem from knowing that they are members of a great tribe that has accomplished many things in its history. Their self-esteem is derived from who they are.

In our society we cannot rely on tribal identity to give us self-esteem; as a nation we are too heterogeneous and confused about who we are. This is one reason many social commentators are saying that there is an epidemic of low self-esteem in our culture.

Paul gives us some help when he tells us, ". . . Do not be conceited or think too highly of yourself; but think your way to a sober estimate based on the measure of faith that God has dealt to each of you" (Rom. 12:3, NEB).

Here Paul is addressing the major self-esteem problem of his day—not low self-esteem but its whitewash, conceit. But the remedy he offers is, I think, the same for all self-esteem problems. When he tells us, "Think your way through to a sober estimate . . ." he is actually advising us to do two things: (1) develop realistic self-knowledge, and (2) have the courage to accept ourselves for what we are. This is the basis for having a healthy self-esteem. If our self-image is distorted, we don't know who we really are, and we are always running from ourselves. But if our self-image is realistic and we know God has accepted us for what we are, we are on the road toward a feeling of worthiness.

How Parents Influence a Child's Self-Esteem

Since self-esteem depends on an image we have of ourselves, how and when that image forms is crucial. Parents are the primary source of information for forming a self-image; they are the mirrors into which children look while growing up for information about who they are.

Children are constantly looking for evaluation and feedback from parents. "Daddy, look how strong I am!" "Mommy, see how I tied my shoes!" "Look at my school report; I did better at math!" When children are unsuccessful in building self-respect, it is almost certain that either the parents have sent the message, "You are worthless," or they have not sent any message at all. Sometimes it is a combination of both.

Sam is the father of two boys aged nine and twelve. His own childhood was an unhappy one; his parents fought continuously and finally divorced when he was ten. He never forgave them for this, and hardly ever goes to visit them now that they have each remarried. He is angry most of the time and feels he is a failure. Although he is a foreman in the factory where he works, deep down he believes he should have been something better—perhaps a lawyer or an engineer. He mopes about this often, and quite unconsciously has developed a strong need to make sure his two boys make something of their lives. But, also without realizing it, he has resorted to an old trick which has been used from the beginning of time by parents who want to motivate their children to do something—he criticizes them every time they do something wrong.

Since this trick has never worked to help children accomplish anything, it's a mystery why it has existed so long. Sam started when his oldest boy was four. "You're just stupid," he would say, thinking deep down that this would help his son prove to him that he wasn't stupid. "You'll never amount to anything. Everybody is better than you." Slowly but insidiously he dug away at his son's self-esteem, feeding the boy distortions of who he really was and thus creating a distorted self-image. Not all the messages were verbal. Scowling, pushing the child away, breaking up projects his son had tried to build—all these actions sent messages as clearly as if they were being screamed to the boy: YOU ARE A LOUSE. But the mirror being held up by Sam was distorted; he was projecting his own disappointments and self-rejection onto his son.

When his second son was old enough, Sam started on him, too. Sam's wife didn't know what to do. She loved her husband but could not control his attitude or his behavior toward the two boys. By this time Sam's two sons have developed major self-esteem problems that will take many years of therapy to correct. Even with this help, some scars will probably remain for the rest of their lives.

Most parents don't go to the extremes Sam did, but many of us through our words and our wordless messages are guilty of giving our children a distorted picture of themselves and lowering their self-esteem. It is important for parents to remember that children can only see themselves through the reflections of a parent's attitude toward them.

Parents who are suffering from a divorce are particularly prone to giving their children distorted feedback. This is because the parents are hurting too; their self-esteem has also been lowered. It is important, therefore, that divorced parents try to be on guard against sending messages that damage their children's self-confidence and make them question their value. Divorce raises enough problems for children without parents' projecting their own resentment, bitterness, and anger on those children. Divorced parents need to be particularly sensitive about using verbalized judgments—words like *monster, horrible, evil, devil, selfish, ugly,* and *no-good* should be abolished from their vocabulary when they are talking to their children. And phrases like "You are just like your father (or mother)" should never come up.

How Does Divorce Damage a Child's Self-Esteem?

Quite apart from the distortions to the self-image a hurting divorced parent may cause, there are a number of other ways that divorce can undermine a child's self-esteem:

(1) *The stigma of divorce.* It is quite erroneous to think, just because divorce is very common today, that children don't experience it as a stigma. One father, in trying to justify his intention to separate from his wife, kept saying to me, "But Peter [his son] won't feel my leaving. All his friend's parents are also divorced." "What difference does this make?" I replied. "It is probably a point of pride to him that his family is still intact. The fact that his friends' parents are divorced is not going to make your divorce easier for him to accept. It may even make it worse."

In Christian circles, especially, the stigma of divorce is still very real. Even though I am a strong advocate of saving marriages, I wish we would not stigmatize divorced people to the extent we do. Not only does this stigma hurt parents; it also causes the children to feel ashamed and less worthy as individuals—whether we like it or not. They may even be teased by their peers.

Help for a child who is suffering from the stigma of divorce should focus on providing understanding and giving support. Communicating an awareness of how difficult it is for the child can provide some relief. Reminding him or her that self-worth does not depend on what parents do or don't do is important. Don't underestimate the power of verbally correcting a child's faulty thinking or wrong assumptions.

In extreme cases, it may be necessary to move away from

church, school, or even neighborhood, to get the child out of a destructive and unsympathetic atmosphere. While it is usually best to change as little of a child's environment as possible, in cases such as these a "fresh start" may help avoid long-term damage to the child's self-esteem.

(2) *Disruption of the family.* When families break up, especially when some children go with the father and others remain with the mother, the stability of the family is disrupted. This creates feelings of abandonment and insecurity for the children, and undermines the foundation on which their self-esteem is based. When the family support system is fractured, there is no longer the same core of reliable feedback that is essential to the formation of the child's self-image. When a home is conflicted or when one parent is absent, it takes extra effort and deliberate planning on the part of parents to ensure that children receive reliable feedback and a positive self-image.

(3) *A climate of love is lacking.* To develop healthy self-esteem, a child also needs a climate in which there is honesty, caring, and a willingness to accept failure. In short, children need a climate of love. Even though a parent may not approve of everything a child does, there should be enough freedom to allow that child to explore new behaviors and even fail if necessary. When failure occurs, love should be there to pick up the child and, in a nurturing, tender way, to point him or her again in the right direction.

Our model here is clearly what God does for us. Without approving of our behavior, he is constantly waiting to pick us up, heal our wounds, forgive our failings, and help us start again. We call this God's "unconditional love," and it is a pattern for every parent trying to build a child's self-esteem.

Before, during, and after a divorce is probably the most difficult time for parents to show unconditional love—although I know of parents in stable marriages who don't show love this way either! A week ago I consulted with a couple who have had a stable marriage for twenty-five years, but whose twenty-three-year-old daughter had gone "completely off the rails." After a long absence the daughter had just returned home, remorseful for her behavior and pleading for a chance to start her life over again. But the father told me, "I just can't find it in my heart to forgive her. I am too angry about what she has done."

My heart wept for the daughter. How could a Christian father be this unforgiving? Was it possible that behind this attitude was a personality that to a large extent had shaped the daughter's problems?

The father said he believed that if he quickly forgave his daughter he would be condoning her actions, and he persisted in this rationalization even when I reminded him that God forgives us without condoning our behavior. As we talked, it became clear to me that the real reason behind this family's problems lay in the father's unloving, unforgiving spirit. While he persisted in this attitude, there was little hope of healing either for the daughter's emotional wounds or for the rupture in the family.

Many divorced parents develop such an unforgiving attitude. At first it is focused on the ex-spouse, but slowly it generalizes to include everyone around. To avoid this, a parent must be constantly on guard against an unloving, unforgiving spirit. Even if the parent's feelings of anger and hurt can't be changed, his or her behavior can—and the climate of love that will result will do wonders for the child's self-esteem.

(4) *The child's depression.* Diminished self-esteem is one of the major consequences of depression. The depressed person not only sees the outside world as bleak and sad; his or her inner world looks that way, too. And this is especially true for children who are depressed because of their parents' divorce.

A fourteen-year-old girl described her feelings this way: "When my parents told me they were divorcing I didn't want to live anymore. I don't know why, but I thought it was the end of the world. Perhaps I was too scared to face my friends—I don't know. The fact is I didn't want to see anybody or do anything. What scared me even more was that I began to see myself as no good. I hated myself, I don't know why, because I hadn't done anything. I didn't blame myself for the divorce—I know I wasn't the cause of it. Yet I felt like nothing. I didn't want to get up in the morning or get dressed or even wash myself."

The loss of interest in life and in oneself is common in depression and it lasts as long as the depression does. If the depression is not resolved fairly quickly, however, these feelings can become part of the child's permanent belief system. Depression after divorce can start a series of events which become a "self-fulfilling prophecy." For instance, a child may be depressed over a divorce, fail to study adequately, and then receive low grades in school. The loss of face over these grades creates more depression and further feelings of low worth. The child's self-confidence is shaken, and he or she may become too afraid to study for fear of failing again. A self-defeating pattern of poor study performance has begun which can become permanent if nothing is done to interrupt the cycle.

Depression in a child should be resolved quickly because it has the potential to create other, more serious, life-long problems. I will be addressing these in the next chapter, and showing how children who are depressed over their parents' divorce can be helped.

Building the Self-Esteem of the Divorced Child

Both parents in a divorce should accept responsibility for taking deliberate steps toward building the self-esteem of their children. Even if the parent who has custody remarries, the absent spouse still has responsibility for this.

My own stepfather was kind, considerate, and very loving. In most respects he was the ideal stepfather. But he could never replace my real father. I needed my real father's approval more than his, and nothing could change this. A word of praise from my father was worth many hundreds from my stepfather, not because he was more of a person, but because I *knew* he was my real father. The absent divorced parent should, therefore, not underestimate his or her role in shaping self-esteem.

Before setting out the important steps for building self-esteem, let me summarize what we have said about self-esteem:

—Self-esteem is how a person feels about himself or herself. It affects how he or she lives his or her life.

—Self-esteem is based on how a person sees himself or herself—his or her "self-image." The self-image is largely determined by what parents say or do; they are the "mirrors" that reflect back to the child what he or she is like.

—High self-esteem is based on a person's belief, gained from experience, that he or she is lovable and worthwhile. It requires self-knowledge and self-acceptance. Unconditional love, the kind of love that God gives us, creates the most stable self-esteem.

—Conceit is not high self-esteem. Conceit is a cover-up for low self-esteem.

With these general guidelines, let us now look at some specific ways in which a child's self-esteem can be built:

(1) *Be kind but honest in the feedback you give your child.* Since our tendency as parents is to criticize as a way of motivating a child, we may tend to be too critical. This is not honest; it is a negative distortion of what the child really is like.

(2) *Teach your child that to be imperfect is acceptable.* Nobody is perfect. The most beautiful people of all are those who know they are not perfect but who are comfortable with that fact. If parents can model this attitude from a child's earliest years, the child will have little problem with self-esteem later on.

(3) *Be careful not to communicate, even unintentionally, standards that your child can't meet.* Unrealistic expectations on the part of a parent can make a child consistently feel inadequate. My middle daughter had a very difficult time during her first college year as a major in psychology. Unbeknownst to me, she felt she wasn't meeting my expectations, although she was receiving Bs and Cs in a very competitive college environment. One day she confronted me about her feelings of not measuring up. I could honestly say that I didn't care how high her grades were—only that she was happy in her schoolwork. My daughter's relief was dramatic. Once she realized I was not constantly evaluating her, her grades showed a marked improvement.

(4) *Build your child's ego with unconditional love.* Even when your own heart is aching, work at showing your child unconditional love. Do not use the withdrawal of love as a means of punishment or discipline. Your child needs and wants your love regardless of whether or not you approve of his or her behavior.

(5) *Work at changing what you value so as to value what your child is good at.* If you value sports excessively and your son tends to be an academic, you are bound to be communicating your disappointment in some way. Try to change your values so you can appreciate your child's abilities. It is a mistake to try to force your child to be good at something for which he or she has no talent or interest.

One minister I knew wanted his son to follow in his footsteps. This desire became an obsession with him; he showed disapproval of everything his son did that wasn't consistent with becoming a minister.

But his son didn't want to be a minister; he was interested in motor mechanics. He loved stripping engines, repairing them, and putting them back together again. Slowly a rift developed between the father and son that could have split the family. But the father was sensible enough to seek help, and gradually learned to see the value of mechanical things. He asked his son to show him how he repaired engines, and worked at developing an interest in what his son was good at.

After a while, the father found that he too enjoyed tinkering with engines, and that he also was good at it. Auto mechanics became an interesting hobby for him. His son never became a minister, but he is a very active layperson in his church, and now runs a successful motor-repair business.

In this instance, disaster was averted because a father changed his values to match his son's interests and talents. Christian parents must learn that they cannot force a child into a mold of their own making. The child must participate in shaping his own mold if he is going to develop self-esteem.

(6) *Help your child find compensations for the areas in which he or she is deficient.* I have three daughters. Two of them have natural singing ability; the middle daughter readily admits she does not. When they were young, not having a talent for singing was a sore point for this daughter, so my wife and I set about exploring her other talents. We soon found that she had natural dancing ability and was a gifted artist. We shifted our values to include her talents also, and soon my middle daughter began to blossom in her own way. If we had not helped her find these

compensations, I am sure my middle daughter would have become jealous of her two sisters and would have been left feeling that she was inferior to them.

Finding compensations is not always easy. It takes time and a lot of energy, but we owe it to our children to help them with this. Giving children attention, asking them what they would like to do, and then giving encouragement as they explore different areas can bring out the best in them and make them feel competent as they choose the areas of endeavor in which they want to spend their lives.

(7) *Correct distorted peer feedback.* Children can be very cruel with each other. A child who is "different"—either in appearance or in ability—can be treated most unkindly by other children. Be alert to this cruelty and correct the damage it does. You may have to say to a child, "Yes, it's true that you are not a brilliant scholar, but there are other things you can do that are more important," or "I know children tease you because you have a limp, but it's because they are afraid something can happen to them also." Teasing is most times a defense against the fear that the teaser could also suffer the same fate. If a child knows this, he or she can more easily dismiss the teasing for what it really is. Sooner or later the fear passes and the teasing stops.

(8) *Teach your child that spiritual values provide true "inner beauty."* Whatever our imperfections, it is Christ who makes us whole. It is the person who feels totally self-adequate and perfect who has no need for God. Our children should, if we teach them correctly, come not to fear their imperfections. Paul tells us that when he prayed for his imperfection (a "thorn in the flesh") to be removed, God told him, ". . . My grace is sufficient for thee: for my strength is made perfect in weakness. Most gladly therefore will I rather glory in my infirmities, that the power of Christ may rest upon me" (2 Cor. 12:9).

No self-esteem is complete without the wholeness that Christ brings. Without this wholeness we are always incomplete. Complete self-acceptance is almost impossible without the "sufficiency" that comes from knowing God.

10

Depression and the Divorced Child

PETER IS NINE. His mother and teacher are concerned that he is not achieving up to his grade level. A year before he was performing so well at school that he was placed in a class for gifted children. Everyone at his school believes that Peter is a child of superior ability and puzzles over the deterioration that has taken place during the last six or eight months.

Peter won't do his homework; he just sits and stares. He refuses to participate in class events and won't talk to his peers. When someone asks him, "What's the matter Peter?" he angrily replies, "Stop bothering me. I don't want to talk to you!" Even getting him to go to school is becoming a major project. He literally has to be forced out of bed and carried to school. He resists every strategy to motivate him and frequently mumbles: "I just wish I was dead."

What is wrong with Peter? Is he experiencing some strange disease? Is he showing the early signs of a severe brain disorder? Examination and testing show that he is indeed of superior intelligence, but that he is achieving far below the level of his ability. It also reveals that he is extremely sad, lethargic, insecure, and entirely lacking in motivation. In short, he is suffering from a depressive disorder. More specifically, he is experiencing a "severe reactive depression"—the label given to that form of depression which is a response to a major loss. It is the same depression we experience when someone we love dies.

What is causing the depression? A few personal questions directed to his mother quickly reveal the cause. Six months ago

120

Peter's father began making threats about leaving home. Occasionally at first, but gradually more frequently, Peter's parents began to fight. Not all the fights were just verbal; occasionally they turned into physical encounters. Every fight, however, ended with Peter's father's threatening, "I'm going to divorce you—wait and see," and his mother's replying, "Go ahead—see if I care." Finally, Peter's father *did* leave the home and file for divorce.

Divorce as a Depression Trigger

Every unhappy marriage, not just those heading for divorce, places an emotional strain on children. The greater the conflict, the greater the emotional strain. In fact, the damage is not caused solely by the separation and divorce itself, but also by the divided house, the tensions leading up to the separation, and the events that follow. Some parents desperately hold onto the belief that children are not affected by the parent's conflicts. Sadly, this just isn't true. Unhappy homes make unhappy children, and every divorce will take its toll unless some corrective steps are taken.

The form an emotional problem takes will depend on the personality and emotional healthiness of a child. Some children are more prone to develop anger problems, while others develop anxiety disturbances. Some will become physically sick, while others will show their disturbance by becoming rebellious. Whatever the specific form of the emotional disturbance, almost every child will experience an underlying depression. For a few—as in the case of Peter—depression will be the major focus of the disturbance.

It is not my purpose in this chapter to deal fully with the problem of depression.* But I do believe parents and other con-

---

*For additional information on depression and its treatment see chapter 6 of my book, *Feeling Free*, and also my book, *Depression: Coping and Caring*, which provides additional information on the many types of depression to which we humans are prone.

cerned adults need to understand something about the problem—what causes it, what its function is, how to recognize it,
and how to deal with it—if they want to help children who are
depressed because of divorce.

The type of depression with which we are concerned here is
called "reactive depression." It is the response of the human
organism to severe loss or threat of loss. I equate reactive depression with the grieving process. Grieving is nothing less than
a depression. It is the normal response to having something you
prize wrenched from you. The depression is the way the body
and mind adjust to the loss and find ways of continuing in life
without the prized person or object.

Why does divorce cause depression? Because it creates a loss
of many things which are considered prized or essential. A child
experiences the departure of one parent as a profound personal
loss. There are other significant losses which we will look at
later in this chapter. Human beings are so created that they
respond to such significant loss by becoming depressed.

What Is the Purpose of Depression?

This question has intrigued me for many years. I am convinced that depression, like many emotions, serves an important function if it is allowed to run its course naturally. What are
its functions? If we examine the major symptoms of depression
we find that they are designed by an intelligent creator to protect us. The symptoms have the effect of slowing us down, making us lose interest in our environment, and forcing us to retreat
to a place where we can regroup, evaluate the loss, adjust to it,
and then return to normal life functioning.

This is precisely what happens to us when we are bereaved.
Whether the loss is the death of someone we love or the destruction of an object we prize—such as an automobile—the process
of adjusting to the loss is the same. The death of a loved one may
create a greater sense of loss and consequently more depression,
but it is not different in the kind of depression it causes.

For a child, divorce will be like a death in the family, perhaps even more so. Death is final. We can't change anything. We are forced to face the finality of the loss. In divorce a child faces a loss, but not a loss. One parent is gone—but he or she is not gone. The loss is final, yet we can hope for reconciliation. Because of this the child of divorce is subjected to a series of contradictory losses and non-losses of which he is constantly aware. This is the worst type of loss a human being can experience; it is no wonder that depression is so common in the children of divorce.

What Other Losses Are There in Divorce?

It would be a mistake to think that the loss of a parent is the only loss experienced by the child. Divorce represents many losses. To help a child through a reactive depression it is important to know what it is she or he is grieving over. What other losses are represented in a family breakup?

(1) Sometimes there is *the loss of other siblings,* as when one parent takes one child, and the other the rest.

(2) *The loss of the "ideal" home.* Somehow an intact home with both parents present has an important symbolic significance for most children.

(3) *The loss of hope for the future.* Children are full of expectations about how the parents will fit into their lives; divorce dashes these expectations.

(4) *The loss of financial resources.* Most husbands start divorce proceedings by saying, "Don't worry, I'll take care of all of you. You'll have everything you need," but end it with, "Now you know this is going to be expensive and I'm not a millionaire, so you will all have to tighten your belts." For most children, divorce invariably means a drop in the standard of living, and this can cause insecurity.

(5) The saddest loss of all for the child is *the loss of faith in God and in the parents.* Children whose parents divorce often feel betrayed. It is as if they are saying, "You received me into the world and led me to believe I was wanted and that you would give me love and a secure life. I trusted you. I made myself

vulnerable to you. Now you drop this bomb on me. You make me feel I am an intrusion. I prayed for help, but God doesn't listen to me, just like you don't. I don't believe there is a God!"

No doubt there are other losses that are related to particular situations. I remember that when my parents divorced I acutely felt the loss of my father's workshop. I was only twelve, but I loved making things with him. All his reassurances that the workshop would always be there didn't help me. The fact was that I wouldn't really belong there. After the divorce, I would always be a visitor!

The Signs of Masked Depression

At the time of their parents' divorce, nearly all children are depressed to some degree. But children do not always show or experience depression in quite the same way as adults. Because of their more limited life experience and slightly different physiology, children often show depression as rebellion, negativity, resentment, and anger.

A good example of a masked depression appeared in a recent case of mine. Sandra (not her real name) was an attractive though slightly overweight sixteen-year-old who showed much promise as a musician. An only child, she was conscientious in her devotion to music; she had mastered the piano and planned on being a music teacher one day. She dated a little, but on the whole did not give boys a lot of attention. She knew her priorities.

But then the divorce happened! Without much warning her father announced his intention to leave the home. To all outward appearances Sandra took the news calmly and without much emotional upset. Shortly afterwards, however, she stopped playing the piano and became obsessive about boys.

Six months passed before the real blow struck. Quite by accident, Sandra's mother discovered her daughter had been pregnant and had had an abortion. Naturally, the mother was devastated. Talking to some of Sandra's friends, she discovered that Sandra had become sexually promiscuous. This apparently was her way of acting out her intense reaction to her parents' divorce.

In the months of psychotherapy which followed, Sandra began to reveal her deeper emotions, and the depression which was masked by her rebellious and promiscuous behavior finally emerged. When this happened, Sandra's acting out ceased. She was now in touch with her true feelings; she could begin to work on them and move toward emotional healing.

Children can mask their depression in many minor ways. They may return to wetting the bed, engage in anger attacks on other siblings and friends, or become more clinging and refuse to leave the presence of the parent. Other masks for depression are marked deterioration of school performance, and persistent requests for an explanation as to why parental separation has occurred. Occurring less frequently, but still serving as masks for depression, are increased lying, telling exaggerated and often bizarre stories as if they are true, obsessive or blatant masturbating, and food hoarding.

The Signs of Depression

When depression is experienced more directly, it is much easier to recognize. What are the signs of depression?

(1) *The child appears to be sad and unhappy,* but does not necessarily complain of unhappiness or even show any awareness of it. Physically and psychologically the child is "slowed down."

(2) *The child loses interest in all normal activities* and gives the impression of being bored or physically ill. This often leads the parent to believe there may be a concealed illness.

(3) *The child may begin to complain about headaches,* abdominal discomfort, or insomnia. He or she may lose all appetite and refuse to eat, or become preoccupied with food and overeat.

(4) *The child appears discontented and gives the impression that nothing can give him or her pleasure.* He or she may blame others for this, complaining that "nobody cares" and projecting feelings of being rejected by parents, siblings, and friends.

(5) *Depression is both caused by and causes a lot of frustration.*

This frustration can make the child irritable, short-tempered, and very sensitive. The slightest provocation may trigger an exaggerated anger response.

(6) *The child engages in self-rejecting talk.* He or she says things like "I am no good at anything." Such remarks are indicative of self-rejection, self-hate, and self-punishment.

These signs of depression can appear in different combinations and may vary from time to time in the same child. A typical example of a clear-cut, directly expressed, depressive reaction occurred in Billy, a thirteen-year-old boy, whose mother was of Korean heritage and had married his father when he was in the armed services.

Shortly after the parents told Billy that they were going to separate, Billy went into a depression. In anticipation of what was going to happen, Billy lost all interest in his friends, hobbies, and recreational activities. He had been an avid surfer who spent many free hours at the beach, but that too stopped when the separation was announced. To encourage Billy, his father offered to spend a day at the beach with him. Reluctantly he agreed, but when they settled down on the sand Billy refused to go into the water, saying that he was afraid something terrible would happen. His father became angry at Billy's refusal to surf, so Billy reluctantly picked up his board and ambled into the water to do a few token surfs.

At home Billy appeared sullen and sad. He never smiled or laughed. Since the separation announcement came just before summer vacation, his parents thought he would quickly get over his reaction as he got into summer activities. They were soon to be disappointed! Billy established a pattern of getting up around ten in the morning, going downstairs to lie on the sofa and watch T.V., then going back upstairs to bed late in the evening. He had no energy, and no interest in doing anything. He spoke very little and appeared to be constantly sad. The impending loss of home, father, and stable environment was too much for Billy to bear. His psychological and physiological systems had no alternative but to set in motion a grieving process— a depression.

Helping Your Child through Depression

While I do not want to suggest that every parent should be able to help a child deal with depression, there are many depressive reactions that can be adequately dealt with by a caring parent. If the depression is very severe, or if your child does not respond to the suggestions I will provide, don't hesitate to seek professional help. Doing so does not reflect on you as a parent. You are not a failure because you get outside help. If anything, it takes a more caring parent to seek help!

The first step: See the loss from the child's point of view. Try to look at the situation from the child's perspective.

It does not help if a mother says: "I don't think that your father's leaving is such a big deal. He never treated you kindly anyway, so why are you upset?" Such an attitude, no matter how it is expressed, only communicates to the child that you don't understand. For the child, the loss is very real and severe.

Parents differ in their ability to interpret the world from a child's perspective. Some are good at it; others simply are not. If you suspect that you consistently misinterpret your child's world, ask someone else to tell you what it is like and don't trust your own perception.

The problem can be further complicated by a tendency many children have to conceal their real feelings. I asked one mother who was getting a divorce how she thought her fifteen-year-old daughter was taking it. "Fine," she replied. "She is more polite to me than ever before. She can't be having any troubled feelings about the divorce." When I saw the daughter, she spilled out her deep emotional unhappiness to me. When I asked her about her mother's comment to me, the daughter replied, "Of course I treat her kindly. I don't want her to know how I'm really feeling." The mother was content to take at face value what her daughter was saying, and missed her daughter's true feelings.

Second step: Accept the child's depression as a normal reaction. By "accept" I don't mean "ignore." What usually happens is that the child's depression triggers guilt feelings in the parent who then, to relieve the guilt, tries to get the child to stop being depressed. "Come on, snap out of it, it's not the end of the world," the parent may say to the child. But this only increases the depression.

If grieving is a normal response to severe loss, then it is natural that your child must be allowed a period of time to adjust to that loss. You must accept this; otherwise you will aggravate the reaction.

Third step: Help your child experience the depression as fully as possible. Whenever I give this advice, whether to parents or to relatives of depressed people, I get a shocked reaction. "But shouldn't we resist the depression? If we allow the child to be depressed, won't we just prolong it?" In almost every case, the answer is no.

When someone is bereaved, we need to understand the importance of allowing the grieving process to take place naturally. "Give the person space," we should say. "He needs to feel his pain and do his grieving." If a child loses a parent in death, it is easy to understand that child's need to withdraw, be sad, and lose interest in hobbies and friends. We would try to provide an understanding, patient, and kindly atmosphere, so that the child could work through his or her grief. But when the loss is due to divorce, we usually expect the child to get over it more quickly. The grieving of a divorced child needs the same careful encouragement and help as any other grieving.

Fourth step: Avoid perpetuating the depression. I have stressed that it is normal and natural for a child to experience a period of grieving during and after a divorce. Theoretically, there is an appropriate depth and length of time which should be allowed for this depression; it is difficult to say exactly how long this will be. But if a child is allowed to do his grieving fully and completely, he or she will complete the grieving in the shortest possible time. The problem is that we usually don't allow the child to grieve fully. Or the child himself may resist the grieving. In many ways, therefore, the grieving process is interfered with, secondary losses are created, and the child's depression continues longer and more severely than it otherwise would.

Paul was ten years of age when his parents divorced. Both Paul and his mother became deeply depressed. Whenever Paul was around his mother and showed signs of depression, however, his mother would punish him. She did this partly because he was reflecting back to her how she herself was reacting, but also because she was preoccupied with her own misery and Paul's depression was too much for her to handle. Paul, therefore, could not grieve around his mother. But she was the only one who could give him the comfort he needed in order to grieve. This created a dilemma for Paul, so he withdrew from his mother, experienced this as another loss, and went into a deeper and more prolonged depression.

Punishment and parental anger can easily prolong depression in a child. So can fear and insecurity.

Children can also perpetuate their own depressions. Their imaginations, fed by fear, can exaggerate the consequences of the divorce. If the child is not kept in touch with reality, the depression can easily be aggravated. Providing reassurance and accurate information can help keep a child's imagination from running wild.

Fifth step: Help your child accept the reality of the loss. Be honest and open. Vagueness and innuendos feed imagined fears. Without being cruel, gently help your child to accept the reality of the divorce. This may appear to intensify the depression initially, but it will actually speed up the grieving process.

Often the problem is with the parent. If it has been hard for the parent to accept the reality of the loss, that parent will naturally have difficulty helping a child accept it.

With very young children the task of helping the child accept reality is not easy. The child keeps asking, "Where is Daddy?" or "Where is Mommy?" These questions should be responded to honestly but gently: "Daddy doesn't live here anymore, but he will be coming to see you soon."

Sixth step: Build a new perspective on the loss. One of the major functions of depression is to give us time to develop a new perspective on our loss. We do this when we grieve over a death, and we must do it with divorce also.

I clearly remember that, when my parents divorced, my saddest thought was realizing that our family would not be staying at my grandparents' country home for vacations. I had come to love the three or four times a year when we would travel a hundred miles into the country and visit with my grandparents. We would play games together as an extended family, listen to the world on the shortwave radio, and pick fresh tomatoes and figs from the large garden. What was going to happen now? Since my grandparents were my father's parents, would my mother let me visit them? Even if she would, I felt, the visits would never be the same again.

Painfully but slowly I adjusted to this loss. My father reassured me that we would still visit my grandparents, but that we would do it without Mom. And gradually I began to realize that what was really important to me was being with my grandparents. This freed me to see the loss in a new way.

An important way to help children develop a perspective on loss is to allow them to talk about it. Someone who is grieving wants to talk about the person who is gone, to relive past experiences and savor the thrill of time past—ask any new widow what her favorite topic of conversation is, and she will tell you it is her departed husband. For a while then, the child may spend a lot of time talking about the absent parent and the time before the divorce. Difficult as this may be for parents, this is an important part of the grieving process and should not be discouraged.

One of the greatest blessings God gives us as his children is the possibility of a new perspective on life. Knowing God in Christ should make a difference in the way we view catastrophe—even the catastrophe of divorce. When parents have faith and Christian values, their children *will* be the beneficiaries. In other words, if *you* put your faith to practice, working to see your divorce in its proper perspective and believing that God will help you work out your future, your child's depression will be greatly helped. It will reassure your child to know that God remains on his throne and rules over his kingdom. Divorce does not dethrone him—it only brings out his power and releases his healing.

Seventh step: Pray with your child. Prayer brings healing. Prayer keeps us sane. Prayer helps us to see things God's way. So pray with your child. Don't pray *at* your child, which is so often how we pray with children. Doing so is patronizing and not conducive to faith-building.

Imagine a parent praying, "Lord, help little Billy get over his sadness. If he was only a better boy he wouldn't be feeling this bad, so make him into a good boy." Well, I know such a Billy. He is forty-seven years old and a top business executive, but he hates his mother for the way she treated him in her zeal to "get God into his life." What was her real message to him? Subtly she implied that he was depressed because he was bad, not because he had lost a father. Somehow he also got the message that he was to blame for the breakup of their home—a terrible burden to place on a young boy's conscience.

So, pray with your depressed child, but pray wisely and sensitively. Pray that you will both have the strength to receive life's blows with grace. Pray for understanding and patience. Pray for God's peace to fill both your lives, and for God to show you how to be loving and forgiving toward the one who has harmed you. Pray in such a way that you communicate a deep and genuine understanding of your child's feelings. I know of no child who won't receive healing from such prayer and at the same time find a deeper sense of trust in God.

Useful Hints

In closing my discussion on depression and children of divorce, let me provide a short list of useful hints that can prevent the aggravation of a child's depression.

(1) *Provide distraction for your child*, especially during the recovery stage of a depression. As soon as it seems that your child is beginning to improve, take him or her on a trip, provide a new hobby, or increase privileges.

(2) *Work out rules that you can implement consistently and with gentle discipline.* While a parent should not be manipulated by a child's pain, understanding that a child needs clear boundaries

and consistent rules, even if he is depressed, can avoid catastrophic complications when a child has "gone too far."

(3) *Be careful what you say around your child.* Put a guard on your mouth. Without realizing it, you can make things much worse for the child. At the present time I am trying to help a mother who is in a panic because her husband is threatening to leave her. "Be careful how you behave; Daddy may leave us," is her constant message to her son. Statements like that place an unreasonable burden of guilt on a child and should be avoided at all costs.

(4) *Respect the rights of the other parent.* Accept that your child needs to and must go on loving the other parent. To sabotage this will create a greater sense of loss and therefore more depression. The child is emotionally the healthiest when there is a minimum of conflict between the divorced parents. We will discuss this point at length in the next chapter.

11

Your Ex-Spouse Is Still a Parent

EVERY CHILD WHOSE PARENTS DIVORCE has a right to go on seeing and loving both those parents. This is crucial to the child's postdivorce development, and it is the responsibility of every divorced parent—no matter how deeply he or she has been hurt, rejected, abused, or maligned, and no matter how guilty the other parent is—to ensure that this right is protected.

Unfortunately, not every divorced parent wants his or her child to continue loving the other parent. In fact, in an effort to hurt or get revenge on the former spouse, parents will sometimes go to great lengths to create obstacles between the other parent and the child.

Of course, this is destructive to the child. Whenever a parent interferes with a child's basic right to have access to and love the other parent, there is the potential for emotional damage. In fact, as much harm is caused by the battles over custody and visitation rights as by any other aspect of divorce. Almost any psychologist or marriage counselor can tell about the damage such battles cause. In some divorces, *all* the damage can be attributed to them.

Why do parents do it, then? I am sure that the average parent would not want to deliberately harm his or her child. When we do something damaging as a parent, it is usually out of ignorance. Or sometimes we have so much pain and so many problems in our own lives that we cannot think about what is best for our children.

Unfortunately, it is the nature of people that, when they are hurting, they feel the need to hurt back. In a divorce, children are too often the unwilling tools of parents who are trying to hurt each other. This is just a part of our human sinfulness. Without the regeneration of Christ's life, there is no way we can escape this nature. If we outlawed custody battles in the law courts, parents would find other ways of hurting one another through the children. Is this not what they do when they snatch their children away from the custodial parent?

What perturbs me most about this situation is that Christian parents who divorce are often no different from other parents in situations such as these. They too engage in bitter custodial battles and interfere with their children's right to love both parents. I could see how this could happen to unbelievers, but believers have no excuse!

The Importance of Real Parents

I think there is universal agreement among counselors that the most crucial factor influencing a good readjustment by divorced children is a stable, loving, and continuing relationship with both real parents, between whom friction has been dissipated and forgiveness prevails. A tall order? Of course. But possible for the Christian parent who has availed himself or herself of the forgiveness and healing available in Christ Jesus. In fact, I would say that this should be the goal for every Christian couple who, for whatever reason, plans on getting divorced. If you can't make your marriage work, then at least make your divorce work—and see to it that you do the very best for your children.

Paul and Cindy, a Christian couple in their late thirties, were having a very rough time in their marriage. Deep-seated personality differences and an inability to work out their conflicts finally led Cindy to ask for a divorce. Peter was devastated and deeply hurt. Basically an insecure person, he was frightened by the prospect of being rejected and of being alone. He feared he would never be able to build a successful marriage.

Paul and Cindy's pastor worked with them to save the marriage, but without success. He referred them to a marriage counselor, who also was not able to break the deadlock. Finally Cindy demanded that Peter move out, and he had no choice but to comply. Deeply hurt, however, he threatened to take the children with him, accusing Cindy of not being a fit mother. Their three children, a girl aged fifteen and two boys aged ten and twelve, became the rope in a tug-of-war struggle. Paul did everything he could to destroy Cindy's reputation with them, and she retaliated with vehemence.

The battle continued for a while until Cindy eventually came to her senses and sought divorce counseling. Without condoning divorce, this form of counseling recognizes when a breakup is inevitable and works to minimize the destruction which might follow. Paul was helped to realize he was hurting the children by fighting the divorce, and Cindy changed her attitude to the point that she could cooperate in planning how Paul and she would continue the parenting of their children. Neither had immediate plans for remarriage, so Paul took up residence a half-mile away from his former home and set up a spare bedroom so that the children could periodically stay with him.

Without hostility, Paul and Cindy carefully planned the details of visits, parenting responsibilities, and finances. Cindy agreed to work in order to help pay the increased cost of keeping two homes.

The effect on the children was dramatic. They even participated in the planning sessions and, by being honest about their feelings, helped their parents avoid misperceptions and incorrect assumptions. The signs of an anxiety disturbance in the youngest boy and of depression in the girl passed away as if by magic and, for the first time in years, Paul and Cindy felt like they were normal people again.

What were the important principles that guided Paul and Cindy to an amicable readjustment of their family?

—Both accepted the importance of the children's maintaining a continued relationship with both parents, even if one or both intended remarrying.

—Both realized that neither spouse stops his or her parenting responsibility just because a divorce has taken place.

—Both accepted the crucial role the father plays in the adjustment of the children after the divorce.

—Sacrificing personal hurt and needs for revenge, they both determined not to let their jealousy and competition for the children's love be a source of disruption in their parenting task.

—Realizing that much of what was needed to avoid emotionally damaging their children was beyond their human strength, they trusted God to help them overcome their hostility and fear. They had the faith to believe that they could do it—and they did.

When a Parent Has Remarried

What about situations in which one or both parents have remarried? Is this any different? It depends on the age of the children and the degree to which the parent who does not have custody accepts a parenting role.

Generally speaking, the fact that one or both parents have remarried does not change the rule that both real parents must continue to parent their children. Take the case where an absent parent has remarried. His or her parental responsibilities do not change. He or she may not be able to do all the disciplining, but he or she must share in their care, feeding, clothing and education, and must work to provide the emotional support they need.

This does not always happen. I know of a number of Christian families in which the father, because he has remarried and in some cases has acquired children from his second marriage, has adopted the attitude that his ex-wife must take all the parenting responsibilities. "I pay you child support, so you take total care of the children," he says to her. He then refuses to look after the children when the mother is away, and when the children are eighteen and he no longer has to make support payments, he abandons them to whatever other resources they can find. There is little concern for the children beyond this point. My heart aches for mothers who must bear the full emotional burden for their children, and for the children who must learn how to reconcile their father's claim to being a Christian with his actions as they make their own quest for personal faith. They have a hard battle ahead!

"I want my children to have a reasonable standard of living and do the things their friends are doing," one struggling divorced mother, who was near the point of total exhaustion, told me. She had been forced to go to work full-time by a Christian ex-husband who had divorced her and was now living with his new wife in an upper-class neighborhood and earning an extremely good salary. His new wife didn't work; she stayed home to take care of her children from her previous marriage. My client, however, was struggling to make ends meet and was on the verge of total collapse. What was her ex-husband's attitude when he was asked to provide some extra help for his children's educational needs so she could cut back on her working? "I have my own responsibilities and I can't be expected to keep two homes." Not only has this man lost a marriage; he has also lost two beautiful children who will have great difficulty believing that the Christian gospel is anything more than a convenient myth.

What about the case where a mother (or a custodial father) has remarried? Does the real father abandon his responsibilities to the stepfather? Perhaps some of these are transferred, whether anyone likes it or not, but each child still needs to feel that the absent parent continues to be his or her real parent. This need is so strong that children who have been totally abandoned by a father or mother early in life often develop a serious obsessional disorder. These children spend the rest of their lives looking for a substitute for what they have been deprived of. Their relationships can become overly possessive; they tend to be extremely jealous and have difficulty developing real intimacy with anyone.

Further Complication

The problem of helping a child develop a good relationship with his or her absent parent is further complicated when the absent parent moves away from the hometown. This reduces the amount of time the mother or father can spend with the child, and the distance between them may set up barriers. It is a fact of life that people who don't spend time together grow apart; even parents and children will begin to feel like strangers to one another.

Financial limitations may restrict how such a parent deals with the problem of distance, but with a little ingenuity a number of ways can be found to maintain contact. Regular telephone calls can be made; having the children live with you over the summer, extending business trips so you can visit them, and taking your children on business or vacation trips are other ways of building close contact. It is very important in situations like these that the absent parent accept his or her role and parental responsibilities. Financial help, advice and counsel, and emotional support should be there at all times. If it isn't, a long-distance parent may find that love between him or her and the children has been eroded.

The "Loyalty" Dilemma

Adjusting to life between two homes after a divorce is difficult and confusing for a child. He or she is forced to make many changes and modify many expectations. The child does not get to choose whom to live with, and there isn't always agreement between the parents about what is best for the child. Sometimes custody battles are used to settle these issues. It is a pity that the courts are used to settle these battles; it would be preferable for them to be resolved through counselors or psychotherapists, in an atmosphere in which the best interests of the child can be taken into consideration.

Whatever the outcome, each divorced child will have two homes and one big dilemma: Where should he or she place his or her loyalty?

At the time of the divorce children are likely to feel more loyal to the mother, who will be perceived as the more vulnerable parent. Later in the divorce the allegiance may change. Parents battle with each other to win over the children's allegiance and to place blame on the other parent. If these struggles are not brought to a halt very quickly, irreparable harm may be done through forcing the child to take sides with one parent against the other.

Forcing children to take sides is an extension of the resentment and hurt that parents feel toward each other, and it can only be stopped by resolving the resentment. This may require professional help. Whatever it takes, parents owe it to their children to get their personal problems solved so that the children can be free to make the substantial adjustments needed to build happy lives for themselves. If parents would accept that every child must be allowed to love both his mother and father freely and without restriction or fear of punishment, the loyalty problem would vanish.

The Role of Grandparents

Grandparents and other concerned adults such as family friends and teachers can help tremendously in bridging the divorce gap and in providing a stabilizing force in the tempestuous life of a divorced child. As I have mentioned, my grandparents fulfilled this role in my life after my parents divorced. They invited my brother and me to come and stay with them as often as possible. Whereas before the divorce we would only visit them over school holidays, once the divorce proceedings had begun they would invite us for weekends quite regularly.

My grandparents' love and acceptance was comforting and reassuring to me. They never pushed me to talk about the problems at home, yet were always good listeners if I said something. They provided distraction from the emotional pain I was suffering and, above all, they restored my faith in God. I came to see that God transcended the paltry problems of human existence. God was there despite what my parents were doing. His presence could not be destroyed by human suffering, and he offered dependable help in the midst of that suffering.

Some Rules for Improving Your Child's Relationship with Your Ex-Spouse

(1) *Stop bad-mouthing your ex-spouse.* Children don't want to hear bad things about either of their parents, and they especially do not want to take sides, since they usually feel that

both parents are to blame, regardless of the divorce circumstances. No purpose is served, therefore, in criticizing the other parent to the children. Don't be surprised if, when you attack your ex-spouse in front of your child, he comes to the defense of his other parent and attacks you back. Children have a keen sense of justice and will quickly punish you when you are unfair.

(2) *Do not use your children as "spies."* A father might try to get a child to tell him everything his mother does—whom she goes out with, where she goes, what time she comes home, and what she buys. A mother may try to find out how much her ex-husband is earning, who his lady friend is, and where they go. No child should be asked to act as a spy. They should be given the freedom to enjoy each parent without hindrance and fear of being cross-questioned.

Children often become very angry when placed in a spying position, and can easily withdraw from both parents. If you are not sure whether you are using your children as spies or not, then ask them! You may be blind to what you are doing and so preoccupied with your bitterness and hurt that you cannot see what is happening.

Encourage your children to call you on your behavior if they don't like what you are doing. You may have to be brave to receive their complaints, but doing so will improve your relationship immensely. Children feel better if you are open with them and nondefensive.

(3) *Do not use your children to carry messages to your ex-spouse.* There is usually a period of time following divorce when one parent is afraid to encounter the other, either for fear of letting out feelings of hostility and bitterness or for fear of what the ex-spouse will do or say. Under these conditions a parent may become cowardly and hide behind the children. "Tell your father he hasn't sent the alimony check yet," or "Ask your mother if you can go fishing with me" are messages that place your child in the role of having to act as a buffer between the two parents. This is disturbing for the child, who usually comes to resent both parents for it.

To avoid alienating your children, do your own dirty work! Be courageous and assertive. Speak directly to your former wife or husband and protect your children from being message carriers. This will free them to relate to both of you without hindrance.

(4) *Deliberately, and very explicitly, give your child permission to continue loving the other parent.* So often I hear a mother say, "But Peter knows I don't mind his loving his father. I'm not stopping him." This is not enough! Peter may or may not know that his mother doesn't mind, so his mother should not take it for granted that he knows he can love his father. It is more likely that she is sending a "mixed message"—saying one thing but implying the opposite nonverbally. We are not always completely honest with ourselves, and we don't always know what messages we are sending our children. It is safer, therefore, to be explicit. Tell your child specifically that it is OK to love and go on loving his or her father or mother.

(5) *Encourage your child to express his or her feelings openly and to tell you what he or she is thinking.* This creates a healthier environment. Now, freedom of speech does not mean freedom to insult or punish. Children are often so frustrated and angry at the world that they would readily scapegoat their hostility on you and turn you into an emotional punching bag. This should not be tolerated. Anger can be talked about; it doesn't have to be acted out. But sometimes parents do not allow children to talk about their anger, and this eventually leads to a need to act out through explosive outbursts. It is far better to allow children to talk about their feelings as they occur than to allow those feelings to accumulate to the point that it takes a volcanic eruption to get rid of them. Start when your children are young, and you will avoid many painful encounters with them later in life.

(6) *Try to be flexible in every aspect of your relationship with your children and your ex-spouse.* This approach can help you avoid many mistakes. Flexibility requires that you be willing to compromise some of your demands and, if necessary, to negotiate for others. The most important area where you will need to be flexible is that of visiting rights. Conflicts with your ex-spouse in this area will always affect your children; they will create tension and interfere with the quality of the visits. Perhaps this is

the unconscious reason why many parents avoid being flexible—to keep the children from enjoying their visits with the other parent. This is obviously not fair to the children! So be ruthlessly honest with yourself and work to avoid rigidity and inflexibility.

The need for flexibility should not be taken to mean that a parent should surrender all his or her rights; to do so would be to invite manipulation. But there are many times when changes are not important in themselves. So don't stand on principle just for principle's sake. Remember, you can communicate Christian love far better through being reasonable than by any other way.

(7) *Encourage as many activities between your ex-mate and your children as possible.* The more time they spend together, the better. It is an unfortunate fact that most absent parents gradually become less involved with their children after a divorce. The initial frequent contact slowly fades away. Fathers are more apt to maintain contact with sons than with daughters. Since both sons and daughters need to have contact with both parents, it takes concerned and wise parents to be creative about maintaining this contact. Personal bitterness has to be set aside and activities with both mother and father encouraged.

When Your Ex-Spouse Is Totally Unsuitable As a Parent

Everything I have said so far assumes that the noncustodial parent is normal. But what should happen if this parent is extremely maladjusted or immature?

At the outset let me sound a warning. Most parents are so bitter after a divorce, especially if they have been rejected, that they invariably accuse their ex-spouses of being disturbed or un-Christian in their behavior and therefore unsuitable to be parents to their children. This attitude usually is the outgrowth of hostility. While it may be true that the one parent has been grossly mistreated, and emotionally or even physically abused, this does not mean that other parent is disqualified as a parent.

The way he or she treats the former spouse is not necessarily the same as the way he or she treats the children.

But there *are* parents who are totally unsuited to the parenting task. They could be advanced alcoholics, criminals, severely maladjusted individuals, brutal or grossly immature people. It is clear from research data that children exposed to such an unsatisfactory parent do not adjust well. In such cases, the parent who has custody may be doing the right—I believe the Christian—thing by withholding visiting rights.

The custodial parent should not attempt to make this decision by himself or herself, however. Deciding whether a maladjusted parent is a threat to a child's well-being is not easy, so consult a therapist or counselor, or talk to your minister, before you take any drastic steps. If your children are old enough to understand the issues, they should also be allowed to participate in the decision.

There are many instances in which an ex-spouse is irresponsible and unsuitable as a marriage partner, but is still a good parent. It is my belief that a parent must be grossly disturbed before he or she no longer contributes something meaningful to a child. I know of one case in which a father divorced his wife because she was mentally disturbed and had to be hospitalized for a chronic condition. There were two children in the family—a boy aged four and a girl aged two—when the divorce occurred. Because the mother was in a state psychiatric hospital, the father prevented all contact between the children and their mother. Many years later, when the children were teenagers, they eventually demanded that they be allowed to see their mother. The reunion was very moving, but what impressed me the most was that both children felt that they had been unnecessarily robbed of contact with their mother. "No matter how sick she is," said the daughter, "I would rather grow up knowing who my mother is and what she is doing than live in complete silence about her. She is my *real* mother, and I need her!"

12

The Question of Remarriage— Stepparents and Single Parents

IF YOU ARE STRUGGLING with the question of whether or not you should remarry, I would suggest you consult your pastor, or a Christian counselor or psychologist. The ethical and theological issues involved are very complex and cannot be set down in a set of simple rules to be followed. Every divorce situation is different, and each needs to be carefully evaluated before advice can be given. It is possible that the real problem behind the question of remarriage is psychological. You may have been deeply hurt and fear rejection again. You may also be contributing to relationship conflicts through your personality style, neurotic needs, or inadequate self-knowledge. Professional help may be absolutely necessary before you consider the question of remarriage.

In one case a forty-five-year-old Christian lady consulted me on the matter of whether or not she should remarry. Together we prayerfully reviewed her life history, her personal needs, her present family situation (which included an aging mother who needed care), and her unique personality (which included a strong attachment to and sense of responsibility for her mother). The conclusion she came to was that she should not remarry. Although this decision was tentative and could change in the future as her situation changed, at the time she was being sensible and rational about her life. She was not allowing her feelings and natural impulsiveness or insecurity to drive her into a second marriage. The risk of failing again was too great!

This is not to say that a second marriage cannot succeed;

many do. But far too many divorced persons, including those who are devoutly Christian, rush into remarriage prematurely, without resolving the needs and problems that caused the failure of their first marriages. They soon find that marriage the second time around does not get easier; it gets harder!

It is not my intention here, however, to discuss the pros and cons of remarriage, either from a psychological or a theological point of view. As with the question of divorce, I want to be helpful without necessarily recommending remarriage for divorced persons. The fact is that many divorced Christians *are* getting remarried, and since the incorporation of a new spouse can have a traumatic effect on the children involved, I want to address the problems connected with remarriage and the children of divorce. I also want to give some attention to what happens when a divorced parent decides not to marry—to look at the task of the single mother or father. And finally, I want to examine ways the Christian church can help the children and their divorced parents—single or remarried—in the difficult task of adjusting to divorce.

Remarriage from a Child's Perspective

Milicent is an eight-year-old whose parents have been divorced for six months. Her mother has become friendly with another man, and about once every two weeks this friend comes to dinner. About two days before each expected visit, Milicent becomes very agitated. "Do you want to marry your friend?" she asks her mother, not once but a hundred times over the two days. "What do you do when you are together? Why does he sit so close to you?" Bombarded by questions such as this, Milicent's mother is overwhelmed and confused. Should she consider remarriage? Her friend has never been married, and her divorce was not of her doing. If she remarries, will her daughter continue to show her protest?

Over the months that follow, Milicent's fears intensify. "Please don't get married again, Mommy. I don't want a step-daddy," is her plea. When she begins waking up at night screaming from nightmares, her mother decides that she needs professional help.

Milicent's reaction is typical of many children of divorce. A very great fear as they face the future centers around having to deal with a new stepmother or stepfather. How a child's feelings are handled when you plan to remarry can have a significant effect on whether your child adjusts easily to a stepparent, as well as whether any permanent emotional damage is caused.

Most children resent the intrusion of another person into the family unit. They are reluctant to accept that the parent has a need to find a new partner. While they generally accept that people need to make new friends and widen social contacts, they don't readily grant this privilege to their divorced parents.

What lies behind this resistance? There are basically three issues for the child: (1) the child's fantasy that his or her parents will ultimately get back together again, (2) the fear that the new spouse will usurp his or her place in the parent's life, and (3) the fear that he or she will not be compatible with the stepparent.

Furthermore, the child usually sees the potential stepparent as disrupting existing family patterns, and he or she resents being powerless to contribute anything to the choice of the new spouse.

Very often, also, the new friend in the parent's life feels jealous of the children. There is a long history of relationship between the parent and child; this may be resented by the new suitor. A potential spouse may also see the children as intruders, because children demand time and take the parent away from potential dating opportunities. It is common, therefore, for the new friend to take a dislike to the children, without always admitting it, and to brand them as "spoiled, demanding, and manipulative!" Naturally, these feelings are reciprocated by the children.

Such feelings are common in the early stages of building a new relationship. Suddenly having to share a divorced parent with a new person creates much confusion and insecurity for an already-shaken child. A wise parent will accept these reactions as normal and will seek to understand the apprehension and resentment of the child. By not getting angry at the child for the way he or she is reacting, a divorced parent can avoid escalating the war between the child and the potential new spouse.

Children of Various Ages React Differently

While there is no "best age" to gain a stepparent, the most difficult age seems to be from puberty (around twelve or thirteen) to late adolescence (around seventeen or eighteen years of age). Very young children and those who are in college or near adulthood tend to adjust most easily. In-between are the children aged six to twelve.

There are a number of reasons why adolescents find it more difficult than children of other ages to adjust to a parent's remarriage. For one, adolescence is the stage at which the child has the most ability to resist change—younger children don't really have the power to resist, and young adults don't have to make any major changes. An adolescent is also more likely to create a protective armor for himself or herself—a façade of toughness, excessive indifference, reserve, and denial. These devices conceal real feelings and slow down the whole process of adjustment.

This is also the age at which personality conflicts are greatest; it is bad enough having to adjust to your real parents when you are growing up, let alone to a stepparent! Typically, therefore, teenagers withdraw and try to escape emotionally from the new marriage. They remain distant and refuse to be incorporated into the new family unit. The problem may be further complicated if the new spouse also brings children into the marriage.

In the age group between six and twelve, the greatest problem is fear. The child is not old enough to face the future realistically, and may demand an excessive amount of the parent's time—either to sabotage any dating efforts, or to gain reassurance, or both. Children may do this by getting sick at the most inappropriate times, playing hard to get, resisting going to bed, or refusing to go to school. These attention-getting tactics must be carefully and skillfully handled to avoid increasing the child's fears. If the suggestions I will make later in this chapter don't help, then let me say again: Get professional help.

Very young children are not fully aware of the changes taking place; by and large this protects them from much of the trauma of change. Provided the new parent accepts the child and an effective way can be worked out for the child to relate to his or her absent parent, the least difficulties should be encountered here.

Finally, don't expect ready acceptance of the new spouse by preadult and adult children (older than seventeen). The new partner will be a stranger to them, so it will take time for new relationships to develop.

Setting the Stage for the Stepparent.

It is generally accepted that the way a previous marriage ended and the success with which children have adjusted to the divorce will determine the success of the "reconstituted family," which is what the new family is called. This is why a family needs time to process and adjust to the divorce before a parent and new stepsiblings are introduced into the picture.

Building a reconstituted family is not easy. All your troubles are not over when you remarry. One study of over two thousand stepchildren, most of whom were the product of divorce, found that there was a greater amount of "stress, ambivalence, and low cohesiveness" in stepfamilies than in primary families. Interestingly, they also found that it was more difficult to be a stepmother than stepfather, and that stepdaughters had a more difficult time adjusting than stepsons. This is understandable, because our culture encourages boys to be freer of family ties and to be more independent than girls.

What this means is that if your remarriage makes you a stepmother to stepdaughters, you will have to work harder at making your second marriage a success. It will take more patience, kindness, and longsuffering—and a greater dependence on God—for you to make it work. I am sure you can be successful, but if progress seems to be slow don't blame yourself. There are many other forces at work besides yourself: your subculture (and by this I mean your church group, friends and the neighborhood in which you live), the nature of your new partner (not all new spouses are that helpful once they have "landed you"), the personalities of the children involved, and the many chance circumstances over which you have no control. If you have difficulty, be kind and forgiving of yourself. Even a superwoman could have trouble in your situation.

Most remarriages after divorce involve a mother with her children incorporating a new husband as a stepfather. Occasionally the father brings a child or two into the household, and very occasionally it is a stepmother who takes over her husband's brood. (These latter situations are more common after the death of a spouse and present quite a different set of circumstances; there is no real parent hovering in the background and occasionally interfering.) And of course there are those situations where the "absent" spouse remarries, and children are involved with a new stepparent (perhaps even stepsiblings) on weekends and vacations.

Perhaps the situation most fraught with pitfalls is the one in which a rejected spouse remarries before having overcome his or her feeling of resentment toward the previous spouse. With this "unfinished business" lurking in the background, this parent is going to have to fight two battles simultaneously. There is likely to be a lot of anger and hostility toward the ex-spouse— anger which will flow over to the children, while the new spouse will not always be understanding and tolerant.

In one family I knew, the fifteen-year-old daughter was caught in the middle of a painful situation. Her mother married too soon after her divorce. She had been rejected by her first husband and—one year after her remarriage—she was still trying to get back at him. Even though she claimed to be a Christian, she could not forgive the man for the deep hurt he had caused her, and even finding a new and loving husband for whom she cared very deeply could not erase her hostility. Knowing full well what she was doing, this woman used her daughter to hurt her ex-spouse. "Go and ask your father for extra money. He is the one who divorced me," or "You don't know what a terrible man he is; let me tell you what he did . . ." were frequent comments from her. She made it difficult for the girl to visit her father, and accused her of "taking his side" whenever she made a favorable comment about him.

But this wasn't all! To crown the daughter's misery, her mother's new husband (who intensely disliked the daughter) would find little things to complain about. If it wasn't some hair she had left on the washstand basin, then it was her letting the kettle whistle after it started to boil. Fighting battles on two fronts like this took its toll emotionally, and the daughter finally had to go live with her father.

Matching Your New Spouse to Your Family

Just as premarital counseling is an absolute must for everyone intending to get married, I believe that counseling can be crucial to the success of a second marriage. It is so very easy not only to marry the wrong person, but to get married for the wrong reason. Before remarriage occurs, a divorced parent needs to be free of any hangover from the previous marriage; the children should have had time to adjust to the divorce; and both parent and children need to be adequately prepared for what to expect in a new marriage.

Since every marriage is different, a set of rules cannot be universally applied. There are a few important points to bear in mind, however, that can help avoid a catastrophic mistake.

The drama of divorce and remarriage has three acts: (1) the marriage into which the child was born is dissolved through divorce; (2) the child and the remaining parent reorganize their lives as a result of the divorce and find new ways of relating to the absent parent; and (3) the parent remarries, requiring the child to make a third major emotional adjustment.

This drama requires time. Prematurely forcing a child into a new family increases the risk of emotional damage. Most authorities believe, and this is corroborated by my own experience, that it takes between two and three years for a child to play out the first two acts of the divorce drama. Of course, children do differ in their ability to make adjustments, so this time period must not be taken as a hard and fast rule.

What can a parent do to maximize the possibility of a successful second marriage?

(1) *Very early in the courting relationship, carefully assess how*

your potential new partner fits into your family and how well suited the two of you are. Complete self-honesty is called for here, as this step has far-reaching implications. If you allow the relationship to proceed too far, you may find it more difficult, if not impossible, to be objective about your selection and to extricate yourself. A sensible decision can be made if you observe how your children and your friend get along with each other in a variety of situations. It takes a little while for friendship to develop, but if after many weeks or months of contact between them tension and unpleasant feelings still predominate, the future does not look promising for the proposed union. Have the courage at this point to do what you think is best for all of you and abandon the relationship if necessary.

(2) *Prepare yourself and your children for the remarriage.* Children need to know something about how a new stepparent feels and how difficult it is to break into an existing family. They also need to be free to express their feelings, fantasies, and expectations regarding the new family. Allowing them the freedom to express themselves not only informs you so you can make sensible decisions, but also gives them an outlet for pent-up fears.

(3) *Prepare your prospective spouse for remarriage.* Discuss how the children are feeling and how they perceive their future stepparent. Also spend time discussing his or her role in the family. Should the new spouse change his or her expectations for the children? Should the stepparent take over certain parenting responsibilities such as disciplining, or should he or she remain impartial? Many serious conflicts can be avoided with careful planning.

(4) *Make time to spend with your children during the courting period and after the marriage.* Your new spouse should accept that you will need to do this. Your children have certain rights and a claim to your time over and above that of your new spouse. This is the price you pay for remarriage.

(5) *Do not spring remarriage plans on your children as a surprise.* There should be an adequate period of open courting so that they can adjust to this prospect, even though they may try to block it. On the other hand, don't introduce a new friend into the family until you feel there is a serious relationship in the

offing. Nothing can be as disturbing to children as to see parents courting a wide variety of suitors, or changing "friends" frequently. If you are not seriously considering remarriage and your dates are casual, it is preferable not to involve your children in introductions. They should be protected from having to meet a wide variety of strangers.

Adjusting to a Stepparent

When a new spouse is introduced into the family, an important series of adjustments are demanded of everyone. These adjustments fall into three clearly identifiable stages.

First, there is the *"honeymoon" stage.* During this stage, everyone is polite to the new spouse and vice-versa. The atmosphere may be a little strained, but no outward friction is evident.

Second, there is the *conflict stage.* Here, the honeymoon is over and reality emerges. Everyone is short-tempered, impatient, and intolerant. Little things irritate, and at times it seems as if the family will explode.

Third, there is the *contented stage.* If the marriage survives the second stage, a final contented stage emerges. Here all the adjustments have been made. The corners have been knocked off tempers and the irritating habits of the new spouse become acceptable. At last, familiarity brings comfort.

Surviving to the third stage requires careful attention to the following points, which all have the potential for destroying a new marriage and a reconstituted family:

(1) *Do not force a new spouse to become a substitute parent to your children,* even if the ex-spouse has totally abandoned the role.

In my experience, this has been the single most destructive force in a new family. The pattern is normally the following: The custodial parent is very angry at the absent parent and labels him or her an "incompetent father (or mother)." Since the children need a good male (or female) model, the new spouse is expected to "become an ideal father (mother) to my children."

This never (or hardly ever) works. There is no way, except in the case of very small children and when adoption takes place, that a stepparent can take over all the functions of a real parent, even when that parent is absent. My stepfather was a wonderful man. He did more for me than most fathers would. But he could *never* replace my real father.

This does not mean, however, that the stepparent should not help with discipline or take financial responsibility for the children of his wife's previous marriage.

(2) *Allow time for the second stage of the remarriage to take place.* Every stepparent needs to earn the right to be a friend to his or her stepchildren. Forcing the pace at this stage can only polarize the family and drive the first wedge into its splitting.

(3) *Keep communication with your children open at all times.* Know what your children are thinking and feeling and you will have no difficulty understanding them. Misunderstanding always has a lack of knowledge as its root. Similarly, keep an open line of communication with your new spouse. Talk about what he or she is experiencing. This will help both of you keep the problems which arise in proper perspective, and it will help your spouse find ways to overcome the problems.

(4) *Avoid taking sides either with your children or with your new spouse.* Try to remain impartial, but privately tell your children if they are doing something to hurt or offend their stepparent, and do the same with him or her. If you keep your comments private and honest, even if they are words of chastisement, neither party will feel like you are siding with the other.

(5) *Keep reminding your new spouse that it is very normal for children, especially in the earlier stages of remarriage, to feel a sense of betrayal that causes anger.* This anger will subside if the parents do not react to the anger with more anger. Try to keep discipline free of all anger. Show your children by your own behavior that you can resolve your conflicts and overcome your frustration without giving in to your anger. Your actions will speak louder than your preaching.

Creating a Single-Parent Family

For many divorced parents, remarriage is not an option, either because a suitable mate is not available, or because they choose not to remarry. Can a successful family be created with just one parent? Can the children of a single-parent family be well-adjusted and prepared for adult life as well as intact families? Most certainly they can, provided the basic principles I have outlined in this book are followed. Two important points must be reemphasized. The first is that even though a parent—usually the father—is not living in the home with his children, he is still needed to fulfill the role of a father in bringing up his children. Second, the way we have structured family life in our culture is such that most parenting responsibility usually falls on the mother anyway. It is unfortunate that this is so, but the working world usually demands that the father be the primary breadwinner, and this naturally takes him out of the home most of the time. The well-being of the mother and the quality of the mother-child relationship is usually much more influential on the child's development than the father's—whether the mother is divorced or not.

The biggest mistake a divorced person can make is to rush into a second (or third) marriage because he or she fears being a single parent. Single-parent families can function well. It is not essential that a spouse be found to serve as a resident substitute parent. Since it is primarily the absent real parent who must fulfill certain parental responsibilities, marrying again just to provide a second parent won't solve the problem.

While it is true that a stepparent can provide some help in a family—additional financial resources, help with discipline, moral support and encouragement, and a shoulder to cry on—remarriage can also bring a host of additional problems. If you marry again, then do so for the right reasons, not just because you need help in being a parent.

The Stresses of Single Parenting

In most circumstances, a divorced mother has to work to provide enough income for herself as well as for the children. (Not all divorced women work for purely financial reasons, however. Many women do it to maintain their sanity. Housekeeping is a lonely task that is not always fulfilling, especially when you have been rejected and hurt.) Even if the job pays enough, it usually makes demands on the woman that take away energy from the mothering task. Personal friendships suffer because there is no time for them. Often a woman's freedom, recreation, and free time are limited to the point that she becomes constantly irritable, short-tempered, and hostile to everyone—even her children.

The single father who has custody of his children faces similar stresses. He has to be sure that the children receive proper care while he is at work; he must do the household tasks after work; and he must provide the emotional support that mothers usually provide. This is not easy for anyone who is not a superman, and it usually means that children must take on additional responsibilities for themselves and for other members of the family. Older sisters become substitute mothers and older brothers become substitute fathers. (This cannot always be avoided and I doubt whether it is detrimental to everyone involved. In many parts of the world it is common for the whole family, including older children, to take responsibility for child-rearing.)

Some of the problems brought on by the single-parenting task can be lessened by arranging for the custodial parent (usually the mother) to work part-time if at all possible, and by planning evenings and weekends in such a way that parents and children are able to spend quality time together. While a single parent should not allow the children to manipulate him or her into giving them all his or her spare time, deliberately planning outings and recreational activities to include them will leave the parent with some sorely needed "alone" time. And of course an absent parent who has been made to see the important role he or she should play in the parenting task can be available to take up some slack when the many duties of single parenting become too exhausting.

Children and Divorce—The Church Can Help

In this book I have tried to show how parents and other caring adults can help children through the trauma of divorce in their lives with a minimum of lasting damage. I am convinced that the Christian church can play an important role in this important task. Here are some ways churches can be of help:

(1) *Churches can accept children of divorce—and their parents—with love and forgiveness.* No matter how Christians feel about divorce, it is clear that children are its innocent victims. I believe that the church, by accepting without stigma the children of divorce—and by extending God's forgiveness to the parents—can play an important role in furthering healing and growth. Such love and acceptance can also serve as a remedy to the tendency children of divorcing parents may have to reject or lose confidence in a loving God.

(2) *Pastors can be more understanding of the pressures experienced by divorced single parents, and can organize support groups for them.* The current practice of organizing single parents, divorced people without children, and those who have never married into the same "singles group" is not always the best way to provide help. The problems of these three groups are too different!

(3) *Pastors can also work at shaping the attitude of absent parents (especially fathers) toward owning greater responsibility for their parenting roles.*

(4) *Churches need to be more active in providing divorce counseling for parents and problem counseling for the children.* Competent Christian counselors are being trained and are becoming more readily available to serve the church either on staff or by referral. It is important for the church to take advantage of these resources.

Divorce is always a painful situation for parents and especially for children. But it is my belief that many of the damaging consequences of divorce I have discussed throughout this book can be avoided. The Christian church, always the defender of the family, can be a means for doing this. The crisis confronting the family in our age needs courageous remedial action. If Christians don't take this action, who will?

Suggested Additional Reading

Despert, J. Louise. *Children of Divorce*. New York: Doubleday and Co., 1953.

Dobson, James. *Hide or Seek*. Old Tappan, N.J.: Fleming H. Revell, 1974.

Gardner, Richard A. *The Boys' and Girls' Book about Divorce*. New York: Bantam Books, 1970.

Hart, Archibald D. *Depression: Coping and Caring*. Arcadia, Calif.: Cope Publications, 1981.

Hart, Archibald D. *Feeling Free*. Old Tappan, N.J.: Fleming H. Revell, 1979.

Highlander, Don H. *Positive Parenting: How to Love, Motivate, and Discipline Your Child to Grow Up Happy and Responsible*. Waco, Tex.: Word Books, 1980.

Richards, Larry. *Remarriage: A Healing Gift from God*. Waco, Tex.: Word Books, 1981.

Smoke, Jim. *Growing Through Divorce*. Irvine, Calif.: Harvest House, 1976.

Thatcher, Floyd and Harriett. *Long-Term Marriage*. Waco, Tex.: Word Books, 1980.

Woodson, Les. *Divorce and the Gospel of Grace*. Waco, Tex.: Word Books, 1979.